Cambridge English for

Job-hunting

Colm Downes

Series Editor: Jeremy Day

CAMBRIDGE
UNIVERSITY PRESS

CAMBRIDGE UNIVERSITY PRESS
Cambridge, New York, Melbourne, Madrid, Cape Town, Singapore, São Paulo, Delhi

Cambridge University Press
The Edinburgh Building, Cambridge CB2 8RU, UK

www.cambridge.org
Information on this title: www.cambridge.org/9780521722155

First published 2008
Reprinted 2009

Printed in the United Kingdom at the University Press, Cambridge

A catalogue record for this publication is available from the British Library

ISBN 978-0-521-72215-5 Student's Book with Audio CDs (2)

Introduction

The aim of *Cambridge English for Job-hunting* is to develop the English language and communication skills you need to get the job you want. Specifically designed for both working professionals and those new to the world of work, the book comprises six stand-alone units which cover all of the following areas and more:

- Researching the market
- Preparing a CV
- Writing a cover letter
- Answering interview questions
- Answering competency based interview questions
- Turning negatives into positives
- Telephone interviews
- Negotiating terms and conditions of service

In the book we have used authentic materials such as genuine CVs and cover letters, which you can use as useful models when writing your own CV and cover letter. On the audio you will hear a lot of interview extracts, from both strong candidates giving model responses to interview questions, as well as weaker candidates making common mistakes. The book will guide you through these examples and highlight successful techniques for dealing with difficult questions, as well as providing you with lots of opportunities to practise.

In the classroom *Cambridge English for Job-hunting* provides between 40 and 60 hours of study. This can be extended using the teachers' notes and extension activities online.

How to use *Cambridge English for Job-hunting* for self-study

If you are working on your own, you can do the units in any order you like. Choose the unit that matches the stage you're at in the job application process and work through the exercises, checking your answers in the answer key. Note down any mistakes you make, then go back and listen or read again to see what the problem was. It's a good idea to listen to the audio more than once and to read the audioscript afterwards to check that you've understood.

For the speaking activities, think about what you would say in the situation. You could also try talking about the discussion points with your friends and colleagues, as almost everyone has experience in job-hunting and stories to share.

Audioscripts and a comprehensive answer key (including suggested answers for discussion tasks) are at the back of the book. In addition, you can find extra material online at www.cambridge.org/elt/englishforjobhunting.

I very much hope you enjoy using the course and wish you every success in your own job hunt. If you have any comments on *Cambridge English for Job-hunting*, I'd love to hear from you. You can email me at englishforjobhunting@cambridge.org.

Colm Downes is a freelance English language teacher/trainer and ESP consultant. He began teaching English as a volunteer in Sri Lanka in 1998 and has since worked in a number of countries around the world, including Spain, Egypt and Poland, and spent two years helping the British Council establish a teaching centre in Brussels. Whilst in Belgium Colm wrote and piloted a number of successful ESP courses, including courses for The European Commission, The European Patent Office and Job Applications Skills. He completed an MA in ELT and Applied Linguistics at King's College London, developing his interest in World Englishes and the use of English as a Lingua Franca.

UNIT 1 Research and preparation

- Identifying the stages in the job application process
- Researching yourself
- Highlighting your skills and experience
- Researching the market

Identifying the stages in the job application process

Most of us spend between 60–80% of our waking hours working, so it's important to find a job that brings true satisfaction. If you haven't found it yet, then don't give up. Keep looking until you find a job that you love doing.

1 a Teresa Fernandez, a recent graduate, is applying for a job in marketing. Match the extracts from documents and conversations (a–h) to the stages in the job application process (1–8).

1 Sending a cover letter
2 Sending a CV/resume
3 Sending a follow-up letter
4 Responding to interview questions
5 Making interview small talk
6 Reading a job advertisement
7 Researching the market
8 Researching yourself

a

MARKETING ASSISTANT, Bristol
circa £25K pa
We are a leader in the international logistics business, with operations in over 20 countries. We are seeking a young, dynamic professional to join our marketing team. You will have a good first degree in marketing or a related subject, and ideally some experience of working in the marketing department of a large company. Above all, you must have a positive attitude, strong creative skills, and an ability to work well in a team. Full training will be provided. There are excellent opportunities for promotion within the department.

b

'Teresa?'

'Yes. Hello.'

'Good afternoon. My name's Alan Cassidy. Sorry to keep you waiting.'

'That's all right. I've been enjoying your company brochure. It all looks very impressive. It's nice to meet you at last.'

'Thanks. Have you travelled far to us today?'

'Quite far. I'm currently based in London, so I came on the train this morning.'

I am a recent psychology graduate with first-hand experience of marketing, customer service and sales. I would like to apply for the position of Marketing Assistant, as advertised in *The Guardian*.

I find the prospect of working for your company very attractive because it will enable me to put my deep theoretical knowledge of human nature into a very practical context in a successful international firm.

c

d

I am writing to thank you for giving me the opportunity of an interview today. Everyone in your office was friendly and made me feel very welcome.

As we discussed during the interview, I believe my skills and experience would enable me to make a very useful contribution to your team. On my journey home I gave more thought to your question about pricing. I checked your prices against how much your competitors are charging for equivalent services, and calculated that with your strong reputation for quality, you could justify charges of …

e

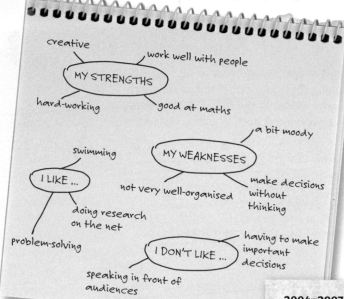

f

'What would you say are your main weaknesses?'

'Well, I didn't use to be very well-organised. Nothing very serious, but for example I used to forget my friends' birthdays or try to rush university assignments to get them done at the last minute. But in the last few years I've learnt some nice tricks to help me organise my life – simple things like writing down all my tasks for the day and not relaxing until I've done everything I need to do.'

g

2004–2007	Kingston University
	• BSc (Hons) Psychology (2.1)
2008	Customer service assistant, Packaging Palace
	• Resolved customer complaints
	• Created customer loyalty programme
	• Liaised with management on pricing strategy

h

'Good afternoon. Faster Forwarding Logistics. How can I help you?'

'Hello. My name's Teresa Fernandez. Could I speak to Mr Cassidy in Marketing, please?'

'I'm afraid he's in a meeting. Can I take a message?'

'I'm not sure. I was calling to see if there are any vacancies in your marketing department. I'm a recent psychology graduate, and I'm very keen to work for a company like yours, because of your excellent reputation.'

'Actually, I think there is a vacancy. There was an advert in *The Guardian* last week. Have you seen it?'

'No, I must have missed that. Do you have a copy of the advert that you could send me?'

'Of course, but you'll have to be quick: the closing date is tomorrow.'

b Put the stages (1–8) in Exercise 1a into the most logical sequence.

c Read the extracts again. Which extracts mention:

1 details of Teresa's work experience? _C_
2 details of Teresa's studies and qualifications? ___ ___ ___
3 the job salary? ___
4 Teresa's weaknesses? ___ ___
5 evidence of Teresa's skill with numbers? ___ ___ ___
6 where the vacancy is advertised? ___ ___
7 evidence of Teresa's research skills? ___
8 teamwork? ___ ___ ___
9 a compliment from Teresa about the company? ___ ___ ___ ___
10 evidence of Teresa's research into the company? ___

d Do you think Teresa has a good chance of getting the job? Why (not)?

Researching yourself

Before you look for the perfect job, write a CV or apply for a job, you need to do some research. Researching yourself is the key to finding the job that is right for you.

2 a ▶1.1 **Silvia Carnali is approaching the end of her degree course at university. She has decided to start looking for a job, but is not sure where to begin. Silvia asks her friend Sophie, who works in the university careers office, for some advice. Listen to their conversation and, in pairs, discuss the following questions.**

1 What is the first thing Sophie suggests Silvia does?
2 How does Sophie identify her transferable skills?
3 Does Sophie think personality tests are very important?
4 What is the final piece of advice Sophie gives Silvia?

b Have you tried any of Sophie's suggestions? Did they work for you?

Your strengths and weaknesses

The first thing you need to do when starting the job-hunting process is a self-assessment of your own strengths and weaknesses. This process will help you identify the skills, qualifications, experience, knowledge and personal characteristics that employers are looking for.

3 a After talking to Sophie, Silvia produced a 'mind map' to highlight her strengths and weaknesses. Complete the sentences (a–j) in Silvia's mind map on the following page using the prepositions *in*, *to* or *at*.

b Complete the headings (1–6) on the mind map using the words in the box.

Achievements	Experience	Knowledge
Languages	Personal characteristics	Skills

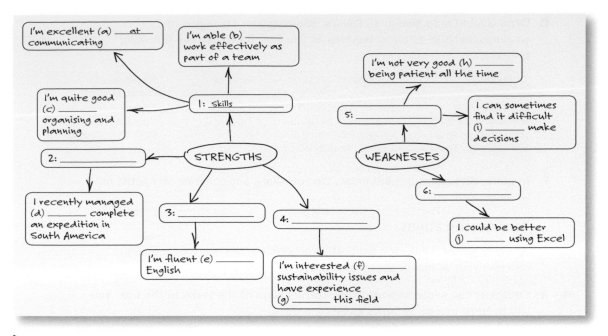

I'm excellent (a) ___at___ communicating

I'm able (b) _____ work effectively as part of a team

I'm not very good (h) _____ being patient all the time

I'm quite good (c) _____ organising and planning

1: _Skills_____

I can sometimes find it difficult (i) _____ make decisions

5: _____

2: _____

STRENGTHS

WEAKNESSES

I recently managed (d) _____ complete an expedition in South America

3: _____

4: _____

6: _____

I could be better (j) _____ using Excel

I'm fluent (e) _____ English

I'm interested (f) _____ sustainability issues and have experience (g) _____ this field

c ▶1.2 **Listen to two friends, Federico and Jack, talking about Federico's strengths and weaknesses. In pairs, discuss the following questions.**

1 What has Federico recently decided to do?
2 Why has he made this decision?
3 What does Federico claim to be good at?
4 What would Federico really like to be able to do?
5 What is Federico doing in order to achieve this aim?

d ▶1.2 **Listen again and underline the personal characteristics in the box that best describe Federico. In pairs, discuss your answers using evidence from the conversation to support your opinion.**

creative	disorganised	flexible
impatient	reliable	successful

e Match the personal characteristics (1–6) to the questions (a–f).

1	creative	a	Do you always do what you say you'll do?
2	decisive	b	Are you good at getting other people to agree with you?
3	flexible	c	Are you good at making your mind up quickly?
4	organised	d	Are you able to plan ahead successfully?
5	persuasive	e	Are you able to cope with last-minute changes?
6	reliable	f	Are you good at coming up with imaginative solutions?

f Make the personal characteristics in Exercise 3e negative by adding a prefix (*dis-*, *in-* or *un-*).

1 _uncreative_   3 _____   5 _____
2 _____   4 _____   6 _____

g In pairs, take turns to ask and answer the questions in Exercise 3e. Discuss your individual strengths and weaknesses, giving specific evidence.

A: '*Do you always do what you say you will do?*'

B: '*Yes, I'm very reliable. I'm always on time to work, classes and meetings, and when I can't make it, I let people know ahead of time.*'

h Draw a mind map similar to Silvia's, showing your strengths and weaknesses. Add as many bubbles as you like. Try to use the following phrases.

Strengths	Weaknesses	Positive characteristics	Negative characteristics
I'm excellent at … I'm able to … I'm interested in … I recently managed to …	I'm not very good at … I could be better at … I'm reasonably good at … I would like to be able to …	I am … I try to …	I can sometimes be … Occasionally I am … I can be a little bit …

i In pairs, discuss your mind maps. Do you share any common strengths or weaknesses?

Your qualifications

At all stages during the job application process you will need to be able to describe your academic qualifications clearly.

4 a Complete the sentences using the correct form of the verbs in the box. You will need to use some verbs more than once.

award	complete	graduate	hold	obtain	read

1 I _graduated_ with a BA in Sociology from the University of California in Los Angeles in 2007.
2 I _____ Economics at the London School of Economics and Political Science (LSE). I then _____ a Master's in Security Studies at the University of Birmingham, which included a semester at New York University at the Centre of European Studies.
3 I _____ with a BA in Hotel & Catering Management from Hong Kong Polytechnic University. I also _____ an MBA in Marketing, which I _____ last year.
4 After _____ from the School of Oriental Languages and Communication with a BA (Hons) in Mandarin Chinese and English in Maastricht (The Netherlands), I was _____ a scholarship to _____ International Relations at the College of Europe, Warsaw.

b Complete the sentences using the prepositions *at*, *from*, *in* or *with*.

1 I started my career _at_ Johnston Group after graduating ___ Hanyang University ___ a BA and MA ___ Chemical Engineering.
2 I graduated ___ 2008 ___ an MSc in Criminology and Criminal Justice ___ Tokyo University.
3 I also obtained a BSc ___ Computer Science ___ Moscow State University ___ 2005.
4 I read Modern Languages ___ The National University of Singapore.

c In pairs, discuss the following questions.

1 What qualifications do you have?
2 Where did you go to university?
3 When did you graduate?
4 What types of career are common for people with your qualifications?
5 Which of your qualifications is most likely to impress a future employer?

Highlighting your skills and experience

Employers will ask for transferable skills or competencies – the skills, knowledge and behaviour they consider necessary for a particular job. Reviewing your previous experience will help you to identify your transferable skills and recognise jobs that you are qualified for.

5 **a** **In pairs, discuss the following questions.**

1 What general skills and knowledge do most employers look for in job applicants?
2 Apart from specific qualifications and technical expertise, what skills and knowledge have you got that make you employable?

b **Match the transferable skills (1–8) to the examples of professional behaviour (a–h).**

1 analytical skills	a I have a justified belief in my ability to do the job. I am able to express my opinion or provide advice when necessary. I am good at making decisions.
2 creativity	b I actively seek feedback on my performance and carefully consider feedback. I demonstrate an interest in and understanding of my own and other cultures. I understand my own strengths and limitations.
3 self-confidence	c I am good at getting a good deal. I am good at developing and managing relationships with others. I am able to persuade, convince and gain support from others.
4 communication skills	d I am able to formulate new ideas to solve problems. I am able to think ahead to spot or create opportunities. I set aside thinking time to come up with alternative ways of getting things done more efficiently.
5 independence	e I can work with sustained energy and determination on my own. I can find ways to overcome obstacles to set myself achievable goals. I strive towards my own targets and refuse to settle for second best.
6 interpersonal skills	f I am good at data analysis. I am excellent at interpreting data to see cause and effect and am able to use this information to make effective decisions.
7 negotiation skills	g I am able to express myself effectively. I am able to make my opinions totally clear and am rarely misunderstood. I produce clear, well-written reports that can be easily understood.
8 self-awareness	h I am good at working cooperatively. I am good at working and communicating within a team to achieve shared goals. I am a good listener.

c **Write your own examples of behaviour for the following transferable skills. Compare your answers with the suggestions in the answer key.**

1 flexibility _I am not rigid in my approach to work._
2 leadership skills _____
3 organisational skills _____
4 teamworking skills _____

d **Identify three key transferable skills of your own, which you have used at work or university. In pairs, tell each other about your skills, giving examples of your behaviour.**

e ▶1.3 After creating her mind map, Silvia talks to Sophie about her university and work experience. Listen to the conversation and answer the following questions.

1   When did Silvia apply for her MA course?
2   What was Silvia doing in Africa?
3   What job did Silvia have at university?

f ▶1.3 Complete the extracts from the conversation using the correct form of the verbs in the box. Listen again and check your answers.

| apply   convince   deal   give   plan   talk   understand   work |

1   'I _applied_ for my MA course while I was working in Africa, and even managed to start doing some research for the course before I came back to England.'
'So you're clearly quite good at _____ .'

2   I _____ for an NGO as part of a large team with people from all over the world. We all lived together and shared a bathroom. The work was quite varied and I was _____ different tasks to complete each week.

3   … our main aim was to educate local people about the need for reforestation. We tried putting up posters, but this didn't have much of an effect. We needed to find a better way to communicate this message. Later on I _____ to respected members of the community, and _____ them to talk to other people in the village. This approach was far more effective.

4   When I was at university I was the communications officer of the student union and I was responsible for _____ with suppliers. I had to order food and drink for university concerts and so on. It was always possible to get a better deal if you were good on the phone. It wasn't just a question of being persuasive though, it was really a case of being clear and expressing yourself well, making sure that everybody _____ what I was saying.

g In pairs, discuss which transferable skills in Exercises 5b and 5c are demonstrated in each extract (1–4).

h Complete the phrases for demonstrating transferable skills using the correct verbs in brackets.

1 analytical skills (*analyse* / *conduct* / ~~*identify*~~)
   a identify a mistake   b _____ data   c _____ a survey
2 creativity (*invent* / *solve* / *suggest*)
   a _____ a machine   b _____ an alternative   c _____ a problem
3 communication skills (*explain* / *give* / *write*)
   a _____ a report   b _____ an idea   c _____ a presentation
4 interpersonal skills (*listen* / *resolve* / *work*)
   a _____ a dispute   b _____ to a point of view   c _____ with 'difficult' people
5 leadership skills (*chair* / *delegate* / *motivate*)
   a _____ a meeting   b _____ a team   c _____ tasks
6 organisational skills (*decide* / *implement* / *meet*)
   a _____ deadlines   b _____ on priorities   c _____ a plan
7 teamworking skills (*contribute* / *discuss* / *support*)
   a _____ an issue   b _____ to a meeting   c _____ a colleague
8 negotiation skills (*change* / *convince* / *negotiate*)
   a _____ someone's mind   b _____ with someone   c _____ someone to do something

i In pairs, think of some more specific actions or tasks which demonstrate transferable skills.

j Identify three of your transferable skills. Make notes about the things you have done in the past that demonstrate these skills. Use the phrases in Exercises 5h and 5i.

k In pairs, take turns to tell each other short stories about the things you have done that demonstrate your transferable skills, using your notes from Exercise 5j. Try to guess which transferable skills your partner's stories demonstrate.

l Think of three different jobs and list two transferable skills that are essential to each job.

Job 1 _____   Job 2 _____   Job 3 _____
Skill 1 _____   Skill 1 _____   Skill 1 _____
Skill 2 _____   Skill 2 _____   Skill 2 _____

Researching the market

Finding a job

Once you know yourself, it's time to start researching the market – finding out more about the type of job you want and the companies and organisations that have similar posts. Doing this will help you make a short list of the places where you'd like to work.

6 a In pairs, discuss the following questions.

1 Where would you start looking for a job?
2 Which of these methods would you consider using?
   • job agencies / headhunters   • the Internet
   • newspapers and magazines   • cold calling / mailing
   • networking

b ▶1.4 Listen to five people discussing job-hunting. Which job-hunting method in Exercise 6a does each speaker recommend?

Speaker 1 _____   Speaker 4 _____
Speaker 2 _____   Speaker 5 _____
Speaker 3 _____

c ▶1.4 Listen again and, in pairs, discuss the following questions.

1 Do you agree with the advice the speakers give?
2 Have you used these methods in the past? Would you try any of these methods?
3 What are the advantages and disadvantages of each method?
4 Can you think of any other job-hunting methods?

Cold calling

Cold calling means phoning a company to enquire about job opportunities which have not been advertised. The phone conversation is used to generate interest in you as a potential employee. The aim of the call is to get an invitation to send your CV.

7 a In pairs, discuss the following questions.

1 Have you ever tried cold-calling a company? Was it successful?
2 What advice would you give somebody cold-calling a company in your country?

b ▶1.5 Eryk and Patrick are looking for work in the hotel industry in London. They both have experience working in hotels in their own countries. They decide to cold-call a number of hotels in London to try and find a suitable job. Listen to their calls and decide who has the more successful cold calling technique.

c ▶1.5 Complete the extracts from Eryk's call (1–5) using the sentences (a–e). Listen again and check your answers.

a *I have worked for a number of big hotels in Poland.*
b *I would like to speak to Janet Robinson.*
c *What background experience are you looking for?*
d *Are you looking for someone with experience such as this?*
e *Are you looking for employees with international experience?*

1 *Good morning. I'm Eryk Pawlak. ___ Is she there?*
2 *I have considerable professional experience in the hotel industry. ___*
3 *My mother tongue is Polish, but I can also speak Spanish, having worked for a big hotel in Spain. ___*
4 *To begin with I mainly worked managing a team of cleaners and porters. However, my Spanish improved quickly and I was moved to reception, where I dealt with customers both face to face and on the phone. ___*
5 *'Do you have a degree?'*
 'Yes, I have a degree in tourism. ___ '

d Match the extracts (1–5) in Exercise 7c to the following cold calling techniques (a–e).

    a   Give just enough information about yourself to generate interest in yourself as a potential employee. _2_

    b   Respond to questions with your own questions to find out more about the company. ____

    c   Use positive questions that invite a 'yes' response. ____ ____

    d   Mention one or two concise achievements, using facts and figures where possible. ____ ____

    e   Ask to speak to the decision maker by name. ____

Job advertisements

A good job advertisement is designed to attract the most suitably qualified applicants. It's not just applicants that are competing with each other for jobs; employers are also competing with each other to attract the best candidates for their vacancies.

8 a **In pairs, discuss the following questions.**

    1   What information would you expect to find in a well-written job advertisement?

    2   What makes a good job advertisement?

b **Employers usually try to squeeze as much information into their job advertisements as possible. However, because advertising is expensive and space limited, they tend to use abbreviations to describe roles in as few words as possible. Write the full meanings of the following abbreviations using the words in the box.**

agency	annum	~~clean~~	~~current~~	curriculum	~~driving~~
earnings	experience	~~licence~~	of	on	per per
point	sale	target	vitae	week	

    1   CCDL _current clean driving licence_   5 OTE _____

    2   CV _____   6 PA _____

    3   EXP _____   7 PW _____

    4   AGY _____   8 POS _____

c Which abbreviation would you expect to see in a job advertisement:

    1   if you need relevant professional experience for the position? ____

    2   if the salary mentioned was for the whole year? ____

    3   if a job agency is advertising the job? ____

    4   if the position requires experience of selling products to customers? ____

    5   if the take-home pay will be part basic salary and part performance-related pay? ____

d **Job advertisements tend to use a lot of jargon, like *proactive team player*. Look at the extract from a job advertisement. In pairs, discuss what the terms in bold actually mean in specific, practical terms. Why are they important skills in the workplace?**

> # Great graduate job opportunity
> Are you a **team player**? Are you **flexible, dynamic** & **results-focused**?
> Do you have **good organisational skills**?
> Then we are looking for you …

e Match the jargon in Exercise 8d to the following questions. In pairs, take turns to ask and answer the questions.

1 Do you have a personality that will fit in with the rest of the team? Are you willing to help with tasks outside your job role when required?

2 Are you someone who wants to work, is prepared to do what it takes to fulfil your job function and make money for the company? Will you be aware of how your actions affect the company as a whole?

3 Are you innovative and creative? Are you the type of person who thinks intelligently and can generate ideas to improve things?

4 Are you prepared to work to meet the demands of the business, which might involve relocating to another office or working extra hours – even weekends?

5 Do you meet deadlines, work well with others and get things done? Can you produce reliable work under pressure and be trusted with multiple responsibilities?

f Read the two job advertisements and answer the following questions. Underline the parts of the advertisements that support your answers.

1 For which job is a university degree essential?

2 Which job places more emphasis on being flexible and adaptable?

3 Which job offers a higher salary?

4 What should you do if you wish to apply for the Media Assistant position?

5 How will you know if Media X is interested in your application?

Trainee Finance Recruitment Consultant – £30–£35K OTE. Queen Careers

Your Profile: Are you a graduate or of graduate calibre with a track record of success? You will have a minimum of two years' solid sales experience and the hunger to succeed! For a trainee finance recruitment consultant no two days are the same, and you must be a great multi-tasker with the ability to push yourself further and further all the time. The right candidate will be target-driven, articulate, determined and overall 100% focused on a career in recruitment.

The Role: The role of a trainee recruitment consultant is varied from day to day. One day you could be sourcing and screening candidates for your current roles, and the next everything from cold-calling new clients to negotiating contracts. You will be working on the secretarial and support team liaising with high-flying candidates and well-established companies in the investment banking sector, so your presentation skills should be second-to-none.

The Company: Very well-established and situated in a fantastic central London location, this is an opportunity to work for a market-leading worldwide specialist in investment banking and financial recruitment consultancy. Professional and consultative in approach, they offer second-to-none training from ground level upwards with bonuses, incentives and fun along the way.

If this sounds like the career for you please email Elizabeth@Queencareers.com or call 0870 12341234.

Closing date: 15th May

Media Assistant. Media X
Quote Ref: 007584 MX

An excellent opportunity to work for a leading international education group in a small but lively media department.

We are looking for a well-organised and motivated graduate to become part of an international marketing/media team. The key objective of this role is to support the team in producing a range of print and online materials for worldwide marketing and sales teams. Tasks will include reporting to the media manager, managing fact files, accurate proof reading and editing, inputting content into our website CMS, coordinating and gathering information, warehouse and stock management and collating and writing newsletters.

We are looking for a graduate with excellent communication skills, accurate written English, good attention to detail and some experience of working in a marketing environment.

Proficiency in MS Office and excellent command of English language are essential; additional languages would be a plus.

Training will be provided for Adobe Creative Suite and Tridion, although any working knowledge of either software package would be advantageous.

Qualification Level: Undergraduate degree essential.
Salary: circa £28K pro rata

Email your CV and cover letter to colm@MediaX.com by May 23rd.

Please note that due to the large volume of responses expected, only successful candidates will be contacted.

g Read the job advertisements again and find expressions to match the following definitions.

1 A Latin term meaning *approximately* used to talk about salaries. This term informs you that the salary is not fixed but may be around 10% higher or lower depending on your relevant experience and qualifications. _____

2 A term used to inform you of the date by which the employer must have received your application. Also sometimes called a deadline. _____

3 An abbreviation meaning *thousand*. _____

4 A term used to inform you that you must quote the reference number when you apply for the position. This number should be clearly marked on your envelope (if you apply by post) or the subject line of your email, as well as at the top of your cover letter. _____

5 A Latin term meaning that your salary is calculated according to what proportion of a full-time job your hours make up. So, if the salary is quoted at £18,000 based on a full-time week of 40 hours and you are working 30 hours per week, you will be paid an annual salary of £13,500. _____

h In pairs, discuss the following questions.

1 What are the main transferable skills required for each job?

2 In which job would you expect to work under more pressure?

3 Which job would you prefer to do and why?

i Many job advertisements request familiarity with certain tools, skills or languages that are relevant to the job. In pairs, put the expressions in bold in order of knowledge and experience required.

- **Proficiency in** MS Office and **excellent command of** English language are essential; additional languages are a plus.

- Training will be provided for Adobe Creative Suite and Tridion, although **working knowledge of** either software package would be advantageous.

j Write sentences about your own knowledge and experience using the following expressions.

- I am proficient in …
- I have an excellent command of …
- I have a good working knowledge of …

k Sort the phrases in the box into two groups.

| ideally you will have …   ~~… is essential~~   … is necessary   … is preferred   … is vital the successful candidate will be …   … would be a plus   … would be advantageous … would be desirable   … would be welcome   you must be …   you will have … |

1 Skills which candidates must have

   … is essential   _____   _____

   _____   _____   _____

2 Skills which the employer hopes for (they may still consider the candidate if they don't have all of them)

   _____   _____   _____

   _____   _____   _____

l Which of the phrases in Exercise 8k are used in the two job advertisements on page 16?

m Read the following job advertisement. Find words that mean someone who is:

1 good at finding solutions to problems. _____
2 able to speak a language without any noticeable mistakes or effort. _____
3 flexible and able to work on different projects at the same time. _____
4 good with computers. _____
5 good at maths and dealing with numbers. _____

Junior Consultant

f futerra
sustainability
communications

Organisation: FUTERRA

Location: Central London

Salary: £18,000–£20,000

Shortlist this job
✉ Email this job to a friend
▦ Job contact details
◪ View all jobs from this employer

Are you a great communicator? Want to make a difference? Talk to Futerra!

Futerra is a communications agency that specialises in the environment and social change. We work with government, businesses and NGOs and have an exciting opportunity for a new junior team member. You'll need to be resourceful and have fantastic research skills, common sense – and, of course, fluent English. You must be adaptable: there will be lots of desk-based research, but you may also find yourself hitting the phones or helping at events. You'll also have to be computer literate and numerate. You'll have a degree in a relevant discipline and a keen interest in communications, and be able to demonstrate a commitment to sustainability, whether through previous roles, internships or student activities. You'll find us bright, passionate, committed and all-round fun people.

n What skills and experience would you need to stand a good chance of being interviewed for the position? Do you have the transferable skills and experience required for the position at Futerra?

o Research the market and find a number of job advertisements for vacancies that match your criteria for work. Analyse the advertisements and identify whether you have the transferable skills and experience required for the position.

UNIT 2 Writing an impressive CV

- Structuring your CV
- Avoiding common CV mistakes
- Creating a strong first impression
- Identifying your key skills
- Highlighting your work experience
- Detailing your education and qualifications
- Demonstrating your interests
- Providing references

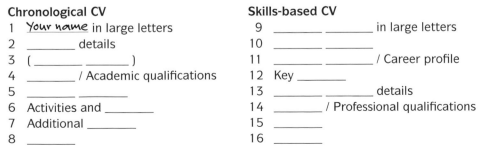

Structuring your CV

You've researched yourself and identified your dream job. You've researched the market and found a vacancy. So how do you put together a CV that will guarantee you an interview?

1 a In pairs, discuss the following questions.

1 What does CV stand for?
2 What is a CV commonly called in American English?
3 What is the main purpose of a CV?
4 What are the key qualities of a successful CV?
5 How many sections are there in a typical CV? What are they?
6 What is the best way to structure the contents of your CV?

b ▶2.1 Listen to Silvia and her friend, Sophie, discussing CVs. In pairs, discuss the following questions.

1 What are the two most popular ways of structuring a CV?
2 What are the key differences between the two most popular ways of structuring CVs?
3 Does any of Sophie's advice surprise you?

c ▶2.1 Listen again and complete the following CV structures.

Chronological CV
1 _Your name_ in large letters
2 _____ details
3 (_____ _____)
4 _____ / Academic qualifications
5 _____ _____
6 Activities and _____
7 Additional _____
8 _____

Skills-based CV
9 _____ _____ in large letters
10 _____ _____
11 _____ _____ / Career profile
12 Key _____
13 _____ _____ details
14 _____ / Professional qualifications
15 _____
16 _____

d Look at the two versions of her CV that Silvia prepared. Which approach has she followed for each version? Which CV do you prefer?

e Complete the following CV using a past form of the verbs in the box.

achieve	complete	coordinate	develop	hold
organise	persuade	represent	research	~~work~~

Silvia Carnali

Home address:	42 Hampstead Rd	**Date of Birth:**	14 February 1986
	London NW3	**Nationality:**	Italian
Telephone:	44 (0) 207 862 4567		
Email:	s_carnali@hotmail.com		

Education

2008–present The School of Oriental and African Studies (SOAS)
- MSc (Hons) Development Studies (2.1 expected)
- 7000-word dissertation on reforestation in Kenya

2004–2007 University College London (UCL)
- BA (Hons) Geography (2.1)

2004 Diploma Maturità Scientifica (58/60) – Liceo A.Tosi, Milano

Professional Experience

2008 Project Volunteer: *Sustainable Solutions (NGO)*, Kenya (6 months)
- 1 _Worked_ as part of an international team to increase awareness of sustainability in Kenya
- 2 _____ communication strategies to ensure that our message was delivered effectively
- Established, managed and maintained relationships with key stakeholders
- 3 _____ local community leaders to increase the level of reforestation in Kenya

2006–2007 Communications Officer: *University College London* (1 year)
- Organised and managed catering for more than 10 separate UCL events for up to 300 students
- Liaised with student council board members, catering suppliers, venues and performers
- 4 _____ University College London at a series of event conferences
- 5 _____ two-week event management training course

2005 Activity Leader: *Concord College Summer School*, Shropshire, UK (2 months)
- Led sports and drama activities for 200 international students
- 6 _____ weekend adventure trip in Wales, including leading a walking expedition for twenty students
- 7 _____ daily meetings with other members of the activity team. Provided training and support for less experienced members of the team

Activities and Interests

2007 Sept Mountain Trekking in South America (1 month)
- 8 _____ and planned group mountain expedition in the Andes, Argentina
- As sole Spanish speaker I acted as spokesperson for the group. Reacting to unforeseen events required frequent revision of plans, responding to group members, tour operator and airlines.
- 9 _____ aims of crossing the remote central part of the Southern Patagonian ice cap in Los Glaciares National Park, improved Spanish language skills, stayed within budget

2003–present Greenpeace Active Member (5 years)
- 10 _____ a campaign against nuclear power. Persuaded 1000 people to write to their local MP demanding the Government to reconsider renewable energy resources as a viable alternative to nuclear power.

Languages	Italian (mother tongue), English (fluent), Spanish (upper intermediate)
Computer Skills	Full command of Microsoft Office Suite
Driving	Full current driving licence
References	References available upon request

f Complete the following CV using the skills headings in the box.

Adaptability and resourcefulness   Communication and teamwork
Energy and motivation   Research and computer skills

Silvia Carnali

42 Hampstead Rd, London NW3
Tel: 44 (0) 207 862 4567
Email: s_carnali@hotmail.com

> *Well-organised, highly motivated communications strategy adviser. Geography graduate with recent professional experience developing communication strategy for positive change. Currently completing Master's in Development Studies with specific focus on sustainability. Fluent spoken and written English. Self-motivated, resourceful and able to motivate others, with excellent communication and interpersonal skills.*

Education

2008 – 2009   The School of Oriental and African Studies, University of London, MSc (Hons) Development Studies (2.1 expected)

2004 – 2007   University College London, BA (Hons) Geography (2.1)

1 _____

- African NGO 'Sustainable Solutions': Six-month volunteer project to educate Kenyan people about the importance of reforestation. My role was to assist the project team in devising and implementing strategies to communicate this message to local residents in different regions in Kenya. To do this effectively, I had to remain calm, polite and persuasive when talking to community leaders. (2008)

- As communications officer at UCL I represented the university at conferences and organised student union events. As part of the student union team I was responsible for dealing with suppliers, bands, etc. and I also worked in collaboration with the marketing team advertising and ticketing events. I assisted in organising and managing 12 successful events, all of which made a profit. (2006–2007)

2 _____

- In Sept 2007 I successfully completed an eight-person expedition to Austral Andes in Argentina, in the south-west of Santa Cruz on the border with Chile. Three months of training and fundraising preparation resulted in the successful crossing of the remote central part of the Southern Patagonian ice cap in Los Glaciares National Park. As the sole Spanish speaker I acted as spokesperson for our group, organising bookings and negotiating the expedition itinerary. (2007)

- I organised and led sports and drama activities for 200 international students at a summer school in Shrewsbury. My role included motivating and supporting the less experienced members of the activities team. I devised a number of sporting tournaments for the summer school students and motivated the children and staff to get fully involved, culminating in an international volleyball competition. (2005)

3 _____

- I worked with a large international team in Kenya. The nature of the project meant that I had to travel regularly throughout the country at short notice, and share basic living conditions. (2008)

- I handled a wide variety of tasks and projects throughout the six-month project, each requiring different skills and approaches in order for targets to be achieved and obstacles to be overcome. I suggested an alternative communication strategy of meeting with local community leaders to discuss sustainability. I convinced community leaders to implement alternative farming methods. The successful approach was adopted by the entire team across the country. (2008)

4 _____

- I researched top international universities for my degree course. I am currently completing in-depth research on reforestation techniques for the African subcontinent for my Master's degree dissertation. Research for my dissertation includes substantial use of the Internet and professional journals, and interviewing experts in the field. I have an excellent command of Microsoft Office Suite.

- I updated and modified the website for Sustainable Solutions, resulting in a 40% increase in website traffic. (2008)

Employment History

Sustainable Solutions (NGO)   2008   Project Volunteer, based Kenya
Concord College summer school   2005   Activity Leader, based Shropshire, UK

Languages

Italian, English, Spanish
References available upon request

g In pairs, discuss the following questions.

1 Why are skills-based CVs particularly popular with career changers and recent graduates?
2 Which approach is more common in the country you are applying for work in?

Avoiding common CV mistakes

2 **a** In pairs, think of five mistakes that people commonly make when writing a CV.

b ▶2.2 A German student, Alex Mencken, has recently decided to apply for two administrative assistant jobs at London theatres. He is in the process of writing his CV. Listen to Alex discussing common mistakes people make with CVs with his friend Ella, an HR officer, and answer the following questions.

1 How many of your ideas in Exercise 2a does Ella mention?
2 Does Ella talk about anything that you hadn't thought of?

c ▶2.2 Listen again and answer the following questions.

1 According to Ella, what words are commonly misspelt in CVs?
2 Why does she believe short, concise CVs are preferable?
3 Why shouldn't you lie in a CV?
4 According to Ella, should you use the same CV for all your applications?

d Ella mentions the importance of correct spelling. Look at the following extracts from CVs. Identify and correct the spelling mistakes (the number of mistakes is given in brackets). Use a dictionary to help you.

1

> In my prevous job I was responsable for dealling with my bosses' correspondance, passing on their telephone massages, and arrangeing apointments with visitors. (7)

2

> Apart form the academic beneffits, the experiance off studing abraod enabled me to practice my foriegn language skills and develope my strenghts in non-academic areas. (10)

3

> During my time as an assistent in the personal department, my main acheivement was when I lead a project witch focused on improveing startegic buisness planing. (9)

e Which of these mistakes do you regularly make? Are there any other words that you often spell incorrectly?

Creating a strong first impression

Writing a personal statement

A personal statement is a brief statement of the type of person you are, your skills and your achievements. It always comes near the top of the CV, before the main body, and presents the facts in the most positive way. A well-written personal statement will immediately capture the attention of the employer and make them want to find out more about you.

3 a **Read Silvia's personal statement from her skills-based CV and find words and phrases which demonstrate the following points.**

1 education   3 knowledge   5 success
2 character   4 experience

> *Well-organised, highly motivated communications strategy adviser. Geography graduate with recent professional experience developing communication strategy for positive change. Currently completing Master's in Development Studies with specific focus on sustainability. Fluent spoken and written English. Self-motivated, resourceful and able to motivate others, with excellent communication and interpersonal skills.*

b **Each sentence in Silvia's personal statement has a different main function. Write the sentences next to the questions that they answer (a–e).**

a What sort of person am I? _Self-motivated, resourceful and able to motivate others, with excellent communication and interpersonal skills._

b What is my area of professional expertise? _____

c What is my most important qualification? _____

d What is my most relevant skill for the job? _____

e What am I doing at the moment? _____

c **Complete the following personal statements using the phrases in the box.**

> confidently and effectively   experience in
> full-time professional   proven ability   well-organised

> 1 Professional, _____ individual. Communicates _____ at all levels; demonstrates initiative and confidentiality both independently and within a team environment.

> 2 Enthusiastic PA with three years' _____ experience. Excellent written and oral communication skills have enabled me to establish a strong network of professional contacts in your area. _____ to meet deadlines and prioritise whilst maintaining consistently high standards. Substantial _____ organising meetings and conferences gained whilst providing PA and secretarial service to main board director.

d **In pairs, discuss the following questions.**

1 How do these statements compare with Silvia's?
2 Which of the questions in Exercise 3b does each statement answer?

e The personal statements in Exercise 3c were taken from CVs written in response to the following job advertisement. Read the advertisement and decide which personal statement you think is more appropriate.

f Find an advertisement for a job you would like to apply for. Make a list of the key points that the employer is looking for. Plan your personal statement with those key points in mind. Think about the following questions.

- How long will your personal statement be?
- How many sentences do you want to include?
- What key questions will you address with each sentence?
- What additional information will you include?
- In what order will you put your sentences?

> *Our client is looking for someone who can fill the shoes of a busy PA for 9 to 12 months.*
>
> In addition to the usual diary management, organising of travel and coordinating of interviews and meeting rooms, you will be expected to facilitate new starters in the department, issue contracts, write up commission schemes and job descriptions and coordinate the company's subscription library.
>
> The ideal candidate will be highly organised and able to multitask. Your written English must be of the highest standard, and as you will be liaising with executives at all levels, you must have excellent interpersonal skills. Previous experience essential.

g You can create impressive sentences for your personal statement by choosing a word or phrase from each column in the following table. For example, *Highly experienced accounts manager with excellent communication skills*. Complete the table using the words in the box. In pairs, try and add more words and phrases to each column.

ability to	broad	consistently high	enthusiastic
interest in	motivator	professional	team leader

Modifier	Adjective 1	Sort of person		Adjective 2	Experience/skills
Extremely Highly	creative customer-oriented _____ experienced _____ resourceful results-focused	accounts manager English speaker _____ recent graduate sales professional self-starter _____	with	_____ _____ deep excellent extensive proven recent	_____ ... communication skills experience in ... _____ ... knowledge of ... range of transferable skills skills in ...

h Use the table to write five true sentences about you.

i Use your answers in Exercises 3f and 3h to write your personal statement.

Writing eye-catching headings

4 a Imagine you only had 20 seconds to look at Silvia's CV on page 21. What would you look at? What would your impression of Silvia be?

b In her skills-based CV, Silvia used personal strengths and competencies as section headings. Look at the following section headings and try to add more to each group.

Areas of professional experience	Business skills	Personal strengths and competencies
Marketing Presentations and publications Sales	Dealing with customers Financial management Managing people	Innovation and creativity Leadership Strategic thinking

c In pairs, discuss the following questions.

1 Which titles would you use for your skills-based CV?
2 Would you use the same categories for every job you apply for?
3 Would you use the requirements stated in each job advert as titles?

Identifying your key skills

Key skills may form the body of your CV (in a skills-based CV) or they may be demonstrated throughout (in a conventional chronological CV).

5 a Look at the following list of transferable skills. In pairs, discuss how you could demonstrate these skills in your CV. Use examples from your work experience, your studies and your hobbies and interests.

- Communication skills (written and oral)
- Foreign language skills
- Intellectual skills (e.g. critical, analytical and problem-solving skills)
- Interpersonal skills (e.g. working with or motivating others, flexibility)
- IT skills
- Numeracy skills (e.g. statistical skills, data handling)
- Organisational skills (e.g. working independently, meeting deadlines)
- Research skills

b The following sentences are taken from Silvia's skills-based CV. Cross out the transferable skill which is <u>not</u> demonstrated in each sentence.

1
> My role was to assist the project team in devising and implementing strategies to communicate this message to local residents in different regions in Kenya.

(communication / teamwork / creativity / ~~organisation~~)

2
> In Sept 2007 I successfully completed an eight-person expedition to Austral Andes in Argentina.

(motivation / teamwork / achievement / creativity)

3
> As the sole Spanish speaker I acted as spokesperson for our group, organising bookings and negotiating the expedition itinerary.

(interpersonal skills / communication / analysis / negotiation)

4
> I organised and led sports and drama activities for 200 international students at a summer school in Shrewsbury.

(organisation / leadership / motivation / writing)

5
> The nature of the project meant that I had to travel regularly throughout the country at short notice, and share basic living conditions.

(flexibility / teamwork / research / interpersonal skills)

6
> I am currently completing in-depth research on reforestation techniques for the African subcontinent for my Master's degree dissertation.

(independence / analysis / research / teamwork)

c In pairs, tell each other which of the transferable skills in Exercise 5a you have developed at university or at work. Provide examples that demonstrate the development of these skills.

d Complete the following sentences so they are true for you.

1 My role was to _____ .
2 As the _____ I acted as _____ .
3 The nature of _____ meant that I had to _____ .
4 Within this role I was responsible for _____ .
5 To do this effectively, I had to _____ .

e Look at the following extracts from Silvia's skills-based CV. What kinds of word are missing?

1 I assisted in organising and managing 12 _____ events ...
2 In Sept 2007 I _____ completed an eight-person expedition to Austral Andes in Argentina ...
3 Three months of training and fundraising preparation resulted in the _____ crossing of the remote central part of the Southern Patagonian ice cap ...
4 I devised a number of sporting tournaments for the summer school students and motivated the children and staff to get _____ involved, culminating in an _____ volleyball competition.
5 I handled a _____ variety of tasks and projects throughout the six-month project ...
6 The _____ approach was adopted by the _____ team across the country.
7 I researched _____ international universities for my degree courses.
8 I am currently completing _____ research on reforestation techniques ...
9 Research for my dissertation includes _____ use of the Internet ...
10 I have an _____ command of Microsoft Office Suite.

f Complete the sentences in Exercise 5e using the words in the box.

entire	excellent	fully	in-depth	international	
substantial	successful (x3)	successfully	top	wide	

g Choose five of the key skills in Exercise 5a. For each skill, write one or two sentences to highlight that skill, using examples from your work, studies and private life. Remember to mention your role, using sentences from Exercise 5d, and add positive adjectives and adverbs to make your sentences more impressive.

Highlighting your work experience

This is the section in the CV where you highlight your professional achievements which are directly relevant to the position you are applying for. As well as highlighting periods of full- and part-time employment, the work experience section may also include professional training, voluntary work, and any extended periods in which your life focused on a particular activity (e.g. travelling abroad).

6 a Think about a job or position of responsibility you have held. In pairs, tell each other about the position.

- What were your duties?
- What did you do?
- How did you do it?
- What were the positive results of the action you took?

b Match the CV approaches (1–2) to the effect (a–b) they will have on the layout of the work experience section of a CV.

1 chronological CV
2 skills-based CV

a With this approach your relevant achievements are listed separately under skills headings at the top of your CV. The names, dates and locations of your work experience are listed towards the bottom of your CV.
b With this approach your work experience is listed in chronological order, starting with your most recent job. Your main achievements and skills are tied to a specified job, at a specified time, in a specified place.

c When you give information about past work experience and achievements in a CV, use verbs in the past simple without a personal pronoun: *Chaired weekly meetings* (not ~~I chaired weekly team meetings~~). Look at the following table of action verbs commonly associated with professional experience. Select five verbs and write sentences suitable for your CV that are true for you.

achieved	compiled	edited	improved	operated	researched
anticipated	consulted	established	increased	organised	resolved
approved	convinced	evaluated	interpreted	persuaded	scheduled
arranged	coordinated	examined	investigated	planned	supervised
budgeted	created	facilitated	led	presented	taught
calculated	delegated	formulated	listened	recommended	trained
chaired	demonstrated	identified	motivated	repaired	translated
clarified	designed	implemented	negotiated	represented	wrote
collaborated	developed				

d In pairs, tell each other about your professional experience using the verbs in Exercise 6c.

e Look at Silvia's chronological CV on page 20. Which verbs in Exercise 6c did she use? Which other verbs did she use?

f Rewrite the following sentences using the verbs in brackets. Leave out any information that is implied by the verb itself or is simply irrelevant.

1 There were five employees in my team. I was their boss and it was my job to keep an eye on them and help them when they needed my support. (managed)
   Managed a team of five employees.

2 I enrolled on and successfully finished a financial management course in order to improve my knowledge in this area. (completed)

3 When I arrived, the company website was only in Polish. As well as Polish, my mother tongue, I also speak English, German and French, and so I decided to write the website information in English, German and French. (translated)

4 The company's database system had a problem, which I found. Afterwards I talked to my boss about a different way of doing things, which would solve the problem. (identified/recommended)

5 While I was working at the hotel I noticed that there were some ways in which the customer feedback system wasn't working effectively. Therefore I developed a new system and put this in place. A result of this was that customer satisfaction levels increased by 20%. (designed/implemented)

g Rewrite the following sentences using the verbs in Exercise 6c so that they are more concise and impressive.

1 I made recommendations regarding the most effective allocation of resources.
   Identified most effective allocation of resources.

2 I was the front-office staff representative on the implementation team for our new ICT strategy.
   _____

3 I was responsible for coming up with the training plan.
   _____

4 I looked after the budget for running the office.
   _____

5 I looked for new suppliers. _____

6 I gave a presentation of our client feedback questionnaire.
   _____

7 I looked into ways to reduce waste. _____

8 I was in charge of the design team. _____

h ▶2.3 Listen to a discussion between Klaudia, who is looking for her second serious job, and Tom, who has just proofread her CV, and answer the following questions.

1 What are Klaudia's responsibilities as a secretary?
2 What skills does Tom relate to these responsibilities?
3 What other jobs has Klaudia done?
4 What skills does Tom relate to these jobs?

i Write the work experience section of Klaudia's CV. Then compare your answer with the suggestion in the answer key.

j Think of a job you would like to apply for and write the work experience section of your CV. Use words and phrases from this section to help you. Demonstrate only the skills and experience required for the position.

Detailing your education and qualifications

If your education and qualifications are your strongest selling point, then you'll want to put this information close to the top of your CV. This is especially true if you are a recent graduate, obtained excellent academic results or have gained a professional qualification which is a prerequisite for the job you're applying for.

7 a In pairs, discuss the following questions.

1 Where should you put the education section of your CV?
2 What qualifications should you include?

b Read the article about how to write about your education in your CV and answer the following questions.

1 Why should recent graduates put the education section near the top of their CV?
2 What term does the author use to mean *just the main pieces of information, nothing more*?
3 Under what two circumstances would you include your A-level results in a CV?
4 What qualifications should you mention first?
5 What should you do if you're searching for employment in the IT field?

Education Education Education

Should your education be proudly at the top of the CV or among the optional sections at the end? It all depends on who you are and what job you are trying to get. If you have just left school, college or university, your education experience is going to be more immediately relevant and should therefore be prominently displayed early on. Your potential employer may be keen to hire recent graduates and will wish to see exactly what your educational attainments are. This means you can give plenty of detail of curricula, theses and grades. However, if you have been in the world of work for 20 years, your education is of little interest to an employer and should go in skeletal form near the bottom of the CV. What you have achieved since leaving full-time education is obviously more indicative of your value.

Another thing to bear in mind is that higher qualifications imply lower ones. If you have only got GCSEs, fine. If, however, you have a bachelor's degree, it is unnecessary to mention your GCSEs, or even your A-levels, unless they are spectacularly good. A recruiter will simply assume they were taken at the usual time and is unlikely to be interested in how many there were and what grades they were. The same applies to a Master's degree or PhD. The higher qualification makes the mention of any lower ones redundant.

If you feel you need to mention more in the way of academic attainment, for example as a recent graduate or as someone with professional qualifications or other postgraduate training, the section should be organised in reverse chronological order, like your work experience section.

Finally, the education section can be the place to mention the all-important computer skills that continue to dominate working life. Different jobs and professions will require you to have an understanding of different computer packages, and if you have good working knowledge of these it is worth mentioning that you know they exist, or have been trained to use them. If you are applying for a job more closely related to IT, your technical proficiencies should have a relevant section of their own (entitled 'computer efficiency' or 'computer skills' or 'technical expertise') much higher up the priority list.

c **What five types of qualification are mentioned in the text? Put them in order from highest to lowest.**

1 _____ 2 _____ 3 _____ 4 _____ 5 _____

d **In pairs, discuss the following questions.**

1 What are the equivalent qualifications from Exercise 7c in your own country?
2 Would the advice in the text be relevant if you were applying for a job in your own country?
3 At the moment in the UK most university students study for three years (four years in Scotland) to gain a bachelor's degree. Some students then decide to continue at university for one or two years to do postgraduate studies and gain a Master's degree. How does the higher education system in your country compare to this system?

e **In pairs, tell each other about your qualifications. Compare them to the qualifications in Exercise 7c using the phrases in the box.**

| something like | which is equivalent to |

I have a Physics degree from Ludwig-Maximilians-Universität in Munich, which is equivalent to a BSc in Physics in the UK.

I have a licentiate degree from teacher training college. It was a three-year course, so something like a BEd in the UK. I got my Master's a few years ago.

f Look at the extract from the education section of a CV. In pairs, discuss the following questions.

1 Why has the writer given additional information about their qualifications (in brackets)?
2 Will you need to explain any of your qualifications? How?
3 What other details has the writer included in this section?
4 What else could you include in the education section of your CV?

> **University of Ulster**
> • BSc Hons (2.1) European Regional Development (human geography and macro economics)
> • 3-month work placement: Economic Researcher, Northern Ireland Civil Service, Belfast
> • Exchange year: Diploma in Area Studies, University of Zaragoza, Spain (economic geography and Spanish)
> • Dissertation: The role of EU funds on regional development in Aragon, Spain

g Think of a job you would like to apply for and write the education section of your CV. Use examples from this unit to help you.

h Look at Silvia's skills-based CV on page 21. Apart from the list of dates and places she has studied, identify five sentences which mention her education and qualifications.

i Rewrite some or all of her sentences so they are true for you.

Demonstrating your interests

The things you like doing in your free time say a lot about you as a person, and your personality is relevant to every job application.

8 a In pairs, discuss the following questions.

1 If you have produced a CV before, what did you put in the personal interests section?
2 Why do employers want to know about your interests?

b ▶2.4 Listen to two recruitment experts, Grace and Oliver, discussing personal interests and answer the following questions.

1 What does the V in CV stand for? Why is this relevant to your interests?
2 What did Oliver think was wrong with putting 'captain of the football team'?
3 Why is it a good idea to list a broad spectrum of interests?
4 What personal interests does Grace usually put in her CV?
5 What new achievement is Grace hoping to add?

c Match the skills and personal characteristics in the box to the interests (1–5).

> analytical skills   creativity   determination   intelligence
> intercultural awareness   ~~interpersonal skills~~   language skills
> leadership skills   resourcefulness   self-motivation

1 Team sports (football, volleyball, etc.)
   interpersonal skills _____

2 Individual competitive sports (cycling, climbing, etc.)
   _____ _____

3 Travelling (backpacking, expeditions, etc.)
   _____ _____

4 Mind sports/activities (chess, sudoku, etc.)
   _____ _____

5 Artistic interests (painting, photography, etc.)
   _____ _____

d Add some more interests to the list and identify the skills and personal characteristics they suggest. Think about what your own interests say about you.

e It can be more effective to present your interests in terms of who you are, instead of what you like doing, using adjectives and nouns to describe yourself. In pairs, try and add more words and phrases to each column in the following table.

Adjectives		Nouns	
active	former	ballroom dancer	rock guitarist
avid	keen	blogger	sailor
committed	proficient	jewellery maker	ski instructor
dedicated	qualified	mountain climber	stamp collector
experienced	regular	Portuguese speaker	tennis champion
expert	successful	reader	volunteer

f Match the adjectives with the nouns in Exercise 8e to make true phrases for you.

avid reader   regular blogger

g Write the interests section of a CV for the following topics. Use adjective and noun combinations, the phrases in the box and your own ideas.

> Active member of   Currently attending   Excellent working knowledge of
> Particularly interested in   Recently completed   Responsibilities included

1 **Reading** *Avid reader: Economist subscription. Particularly interested in reading about recent developments in science and technology.*

2 **Walking** _____

3 **Photography** _____

4 **University Social Coordinator** _____

h Write sentences about your own interests. Be as specific as possible and highlight the skills you need to achieve the things you enjoy doing.

i In pairs, take turns to talk about your personal interests. Start with the question, '*So what do you like doing in your free time?*' Encourage your partner to highlight the skills that their personal interests demonstrate.

j Think of a specific job you want to apply for and write the interests section of your CV. Highlight the skills that are relevant for the job.

Providing references

References provide further evidence to potential future employers that you are who you say you are, and that you have done what you claim to have done for previous employers. It is highly likely that your referees will be contacted if you are shortlisted, so it is essential to select them carefully.

9 a In pairs, discuss the following questions.

1 Why are references important?
2 How many referees do you need, and who should you choose?
3 When is a referee no longer useful?
4 What happens if you don't get on with the most obvious choices for your referees?
5 Is it OK to use someone you know well who works for the organisation where you are applying for a job?
6 Do you have to give your current employer?
7 How can you find out what a reference says about you?

b Match the questions (1–7) in Exercise 9a to the following expert advice (a–g). Do you agree with the advice?

a Usually two – an academic one and either an employer or a personal/ character referee. They should be of professional standing so that they can comment on your suitability for the job. Do not use a relative; a family friend is OK. Always ask permission before using someone as a reference. Provide them with a copy of your CV and an indication of the jobs you are applying for. Let them know how you got on, and thank them afterwards. **2**

b Yes, but they may feel uncomfortable, so be sensitive. They are putting their reputation on the line. ___

c You can't easily – that's the point of a confidential reference. If you suspect a poor reference is causing you problems, try changing your referee. ___

d It is normal to ask for your current employer not to be contacted yet. Offer another referee. Ask to be alerted before your employer is contacted. ___

e When they don't remember who you are or become uncontactable. ___

f Choose another who will represent you in the best light. ___

g References provide confidential information about your character, skills and experience. A positive recommendation will greatly support your application. ___

c In pairs, discuss the following statements. Do you agree with them?

1 It is better to choose professional or academic referees than personal friends.
2 As long as your references back up the facts on your CV, then you don't need to worry.
3 You don't need to provide the names and contact details of your referees in your CV.

d ▶2.5 The opinions in Exercise 9c are expressed by the recruitment consultants, Grace and Oliver, in a discussion about providing references. Listen to the conversation and answer the following questions.

1 Who expressed which opinion (1–3)? Write O (Oliver), G (Grace) or B (Both).
2 What reasons did they give in support of their opinions?
3 What phrase does Oliver use to say you can provide references if they are needed?

e Think of a specific job you would like to apply for and, using the models presented in this unit, write your CV. Remember to highlight only your skills and experience that are relevant for a job.

f In pairs, evaluate each other's CVs. Think about the following questions.

● Is the English natural and accurate?
● Does everything make sense? Do you get a good idea of your partner's life by reading their CV?
● Is the language impressive and persuasive? If not, how can you improve it?
● Is the layout attractive and logical? If not, how can you improve it?
● Does your partner's CV demonstrate a wide range of transferable skills? If not, where could you add more proof?
● Does your partner's CV demonstrate that your partner is suitable for the job they want? If not, why not?
● Is the CV too long? If so, which words/sentences/sections would you delete or edit?

When you are happy with the feedback you have received, rewrite your CV. Repeat the process until your CV is perfect.

- Identifying features of cover letters
- Beginning a cover letter
- Writing the main body of the letter
- Writing an effective final paragraph
- Using appropriate language
- Writing a cover letter

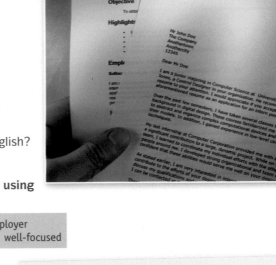

Identifying features of cover letters

1 a In pairs, discuss the following questions.

1 What's the difference between a CV and a cover letter?
2 Have you ever written a cover letter in English?
3 What did you write in your cover letter?

b Complete this introduction to cover letters using the words in the box.

| business | complement | cover letter | CV | employer |
| interview | introduction | persuade | position | well-focused |

c Find an alternative expression for cover letter in the text.

d Vicky Tang is the Communications Manager at Green Pharmaceuticals. She wants to change her job and phones her friend, Felix, a recruitment agent, for advice on writing a cover letter. In pairs, discuss what advice you would give Vicky on the following areas.

- the length and structure of the letter
- the language you would use
- the content of the letter

e ▶ 3.1 Listen to the beginning of the phone call and answer the following questions.

1 How long has Vicky been working at Green Pharmaceuticals?
2 Why is Vicky looking for a new job?

What is a cover letter?

A (1) ___CV___ gives information about the educational qualifications and professional experience you have, whereas a (2) _____ explains why you want the job. A cover letter should (3) _____ , not duplicate, your CV. The main purpose of a personalised cover letter is to (4) _____ the reader to read your CV and consider you for the vacant (5) _____ .

A cover letter is often your earliest written contact with a potential (6) _____ , creating a critical first impression. A well-written, (7) _____ cover letter demonstrates your written communication skills and will help you to get that all-important (8) _____ .

The letter of application should follow the general guidelines for all (9) _____ letters. It should have an (10) _____ , a main body, and a final paragraph.

f ▶3.2 **Read the statements below and predict whether Felix recommends them (✔) or not (✗). Listen to the rest of the conversation and check your answers.**

1 Use high-quality paper that matches the paper of your CV. ✔
2 Ensure that your cover letter is written using formal language.
3 Use the same cover letter for every application.
4 Show that you have done some research into the company you are applying to.
5 Emphasise your suitability for the post.
6 Enclose copies of your educational qualifications and certificates.

g **What do you think is the most important advice that Felix gives Vicky?**

h **Look at the example of a good cover letter that Felix sent Vicky. Read the letter and answer the following questions.**

1 What is Jane studying at university?
2 Where did she work last summer?
3 What does she do in her free time?

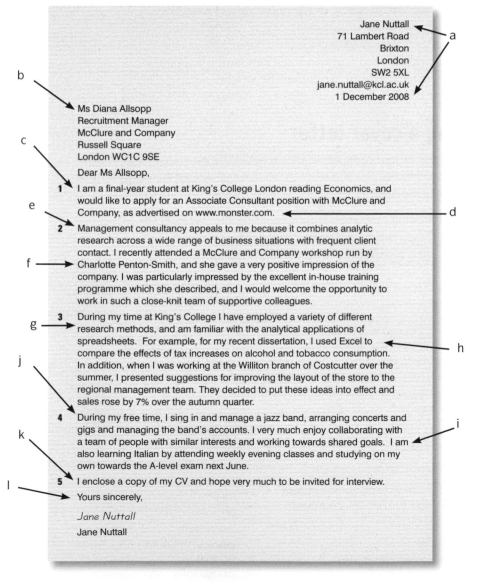

a

Jane Nuttall
71 Lambert Road
Brixton
London
SW2 5XL
jane.nuttall@kcl.ac.uk
1 December 2008

b

Ms Diana Allsopp
Recruitment Manager
McClure and Company
Russell Square
London WC1C 9SE

c

Dear Ms Allsopp,

1 I am a final-year student at King's College London reading Economics, and would like to apply for an Associate Consultant position with McClure and Company, as advertised on www.monster.com. ← d

e

2 Management consultancy appeals to me because it combines analytic research across a wide range of business situations with frequent client contact. I recently attended a McClure and Company workshop run by Charlotte Penton-Smith, and she gave a very positive impression of the company. I was particularly impressed by the excellent in-house training programme which she described, and I would welcome the opportunity to work in such a close-knit team of supportive colleagues.

f

3 During my time at King's College I have employed a variety of different research methods, and am familiar with the analytical applications of spreadsheets. For example, for my recent dissertation, I used Excel to compare the effects of tax increases on alcohol and tobacco consumption. In addition, when I was working at the Williton branch of Costcutter over the summer, I presented suggestions for improving the layout of the store to the regional management team. They decided to put these ideas into effect and sales rose by 7% over the autumn quarter.

g   h

j

4 During my free time, I sing in and manage a jazz band, arranging concerts and gigs and managing the band's accounts. I very much enjoy collaborating with a team of people with similar interests and working towards shared goals. I am also learning Italian by attending weekly evening classes and studying on my own towards the A-level exam next June.

k   i

5 I enclose a copy of my CV and hope very much to be invited for interview.

l

Yours sincerely,

Jane Nuttall

Jane Nuttall

i Match Felix's advice (1–12) to the parts of the cover letter (a–l) in Exercise 1h.

1 Give your contact information and current date. _a_
2 End 'Yours sincerely' and type your name under your signature (indicate Ms or Mr if not obvious). ___
3 Give a clear context – say who you are and why you are writing. ___
4 Your sign-off should be friendly, polite and to the point. ___
5 Point out your aptitude for the sorts of skills they are seeking. ___
6 Name any employee you have met and say why they impressed you. ___
7 Your use of leisure time can show you are a well-rounded person. ___
8 Support your claims with evidence, focusing on results and achievements. ___
9 Include the name, title and full address of recipient. ___
10 Mention where you saw the job advertisement. ___
11 Explain your motivation for applying. This also shows you have done your research and learned something about the sector. ___
12 Show you are acquiring additional useful skills. ___

j Look at Jane's cover letter again. In which paragraph does she:

1 explain her interest in the position? ___
2 create a positive final impression? ___
3 demonstrate her skills and experience relevant for the position? ___
4 introduce herself and explain her reasons for writing? ___
5 mention other relevant skills and interests to impress the employer? ___

Beginning a cover letter

The first paragraph of your cover letter should detail the job you are applying for and, if relevant, where you heard about the job (for example an advertisement, or personal recommendation).

2 a Complete the following opening paragraphs using the words in the box.

advertised	application	consideration	enclosed	enquire
graduate	qualified	recommended	requirements	response

1 I am a final-year student who is about to __graduate__ with a bachelor's degree in Industrial Engineering from Bristol University. I am writing to _____ about possible employment opportunities with Mendoza. I am interested in a position related to transportation management.

2 I am writing in _____ to your job posting for an investment banker on your company's website. I have _____ my CV for your consideration.

3 I was recently speaking with Mr Fox from your firm and he _____ that I send you a copy of my CV. Knowing the _____ for the position, he felt that I would be an ideal candidate, given my experience in international sales.

4 I would like to apply for the post of a Commercial Solicitor in your firm as _____ on Legalpositions.com. As a recent graduate, I was particularly happy to see that the position is open to newly _____ lawyers.

5 Please accept this letter as _____ for the Marketing Manager position currently listed on Monster.com. My CV is attached for your _____ .

b Match the opening paragraphs (1–5) in Exercise 2a to the type of cover letter (a–c) they come from. Which type of letter do you think is most likely to be successful?

a A reply to a job advertisement
b A 'cold' speculative job application
c A letter following a personal recommendation

c Evaluate the following opening paragraphs. What do you think is good or bad about them?

1 After attending the recruitment talk presented by Financial Investments, I am extremely interested in the post of graduate trainee in the International Sales Department. I have absolutely no doubt that my qualifications, skills and professional experience will make me an indispensable member of your team.

2 I am writing to apply for the graduate trainee position as advertised online in the *New York Times*. I am a final-year student majoring in Business Administration, with US and Chinese business relations as the focus of my dissertation. I believe I am suitable for this position because I am very interested in banking.

3 I would like to apply for a job in your organisation. I have always wanted to work at the cutting edge of global strategy with a firm whose greatest assets are its people, and I have decided that Rivers & Co. is the ideal place to start my career.

d ▶3.3 Listen to two recruitment experts, Grace and Oliver, discussing the letters. In which order do they discuss them?

e ▶3.3 Listen again. What advice do they give? Do you agree with their comments?

f Find a job advertisement that interests you, and write the opening paragraph of a cover letter in response.

Writing the main body of the letter

Demonstrating your key skills and experience

In the main body of the letter you need to show why you are the right person for the job, by highlighting your most relevant experiences and skills as they relate to the position you are applying for. It is important to demonstrate evidence of your skills clearly. It is not enough to claim that you are 'a hard-working, flexible team player, with excellent IT skills'; you need to be able to provide evidence.

3 a In pairs, discuss the following questions.

1 How long should the main body of the letter be?
2 How many specific points should you make?
3 How will this section change depending on the job you are applying for?

b Read the following extracts from cover letters. For each extract underline the two main skills the applicants demonstrate.

1

> My past experience of working overseas has brought me a greater understanding of international cultures and traditions, as well as a better appreciation of my own culture. These insights would certainly benefit a multinational corporation, such as yours.

Skills: <u>intercultural awareness</u> / dependability / flexibility / <u>self-awareness</u>

2

> Within my role as a project manager, I am responsible for leading a team of five people. We often have to work unsociable hours under difficult conditions. I ensure that team morale is maintained by regularly counselling team members to check they are coping with the demands of the job.

Skills: flexibility / lateral thinking skills / language skills / interpersonal skills

3

> Although I do not possess any experience in the hotel industry, I was a Holiday Representative for Xtreme Holidays for two consecutive summers, where I learned that customer satisfaction is the key to success in the service industry. I implemented a new way for customer feedback to be recorded, which helped Xtreme Holidays develop the service that they provide by identifying areas needing improvement. I believe I can apply the skills obtained from my previous employment to this position.

Skills: IT skills / customer service skills / communication skills / initiative

4

> This summer I worked at Alton Towers Themepark, where I was initially responsible for operating various rides. However, as I can speak both Italian and English fluently I was quickly moved into the gift shop to deal with customers. Working in the shop helped me to learn the importance of dealing with customers in a friendly and efficient way. During this month I suggested changing the layout of some of the gift displays. These changes led to a significant increase in the sales of souvenirs.

Skills: customer service skills / entrepreneurial skills / leadership skills / numerical skills

5

> I have a strong history of staff management, working closely with my current team on their personal development plans, and understand my role assisting and promoting staff member success. I regularly seek feedback on my performance from my superiors and colleagues to identify areas I need to improve in.

Skills: reliability / leadership skills / self-awareness / technical skills

c Underline useful phrases from the extracts which you could use in your own cover letter. For example in extract 1, *My past experience of* … *has brought me a greater understanding of* …, *as well as* …

d Identify three skills that you use on a regular basis and write three sentences that demonstrate these skills in action. Use the phrases in Exercise 3c to help you.

Matching your skills and experience to the position

In the body of your cover letter it is essential that you are able to demonstrate how your work experience and skills match the specific position you are applying for. To do this you need to:

- read the job description carefully;
- identify the skills and experience the company is particularly interested in;
- show any parallels with previous posts you have held or other experience.

4 a In pairs, discuss the following questions.

1 How will your cover letter change with each position you apply for?
2 How will you know which skills and experience to highlight?
3 Should you highlight skills and experience even if they are not obviously relevant to the job you are applying for?

b Read the letter written by Hanna Ahigren, who is applying for a job at the Australian Embassy in Sweden, and answer the following questions. At this stage, ignore the gaps in the text.

1 What position is Hanna applying for?
2 What is her current job?
3 What subject does she have a degree in?
4 What skills and experience does she have?

Dear Ms Tisdall,

I am writing in response to your advertisement for the position of Public Relations Officer and enclose my curriculum vitae for your consideration.

I am currently working as a Press Officer for the Swedish Ministry of Industry. (1) _This experience has enabled me to_ gain a broad understanding of the media and public relations. (2) _____ monitoring the Swedish and foreign media, and establishing and maintaining key media contacts. I also write press releases and organise media events. Through the successful undertaking of these responsibilities (3) _____ the Swedish political system. (4) _____ theoretical knowledge attained as part of my university degree in Political Science, and put this knowledge into practical application.

Previous experience at the Swedish Embassy in Warsaw gave me an opportunity to work with the diplomatic services. During my time there I learnt to promote the strengths of Sweden through public relations events, as part of a team. Poland's entry to the European Union was the main focus of the Embassy at the time, which significantly influenced my work there. (5) _____ writing reports, organising official visits to Poland, and developing various internal and external projects.

(6) _____ considerable experience in the area of public relations from my years at university and subsequent jobs. I am confident that the combination of my political science background and relevant skills makes me an ideal candidate for the position available. (7) _____ ideas and enthusiasm to the job.

(8) _____ I am very suited to Embassy work and feel this move would be a logical career step. The role of Public Relations Officer would allow me to develop my existing skills in an environment in which my political, linguistic and diplomatic skills could be utilised to their greatest potential.

I would be available for interview at your convenience. I look forward to hearing from you.

Yours sincerely,

Hanna Ahigren

Ms Hanna Ahigren

c Complete the letter in Exercise 4b using the following phrases.

a I feel I have significantly strengthened my knowledge and understanding of
b ~~This experience has enabled me to~~
c My employment experience leads me to the conclusion that
d My employment experience has enabled me to build on
e I think that I could bring
f My responsibilities included
g Within my position at work I am responsible for
h As you can see from my CV I have

d Here is the advertisement that Hanna responded to. In pairs, identify the main skills and experience they are looking for.

e Match the requirements listed in the advertisement (a–i) to sentences from Hanna's cover letter (1–6). Some sentences illustrate more than one requirement.

1 This experience has enabled me to gain a broad understanding of the media and public relations. _i_

2 Within my position at work I am responsible for monitoring the Swedish and foreign media, and establishing and maintaining key media contacts.
___ / ___ / ___

3 Through the successful undertaking of these responsibilities I feel I have significantly strengthened my knowledge and understanding of the Swedish political system. ___

4 Previous experience at the Swedish Embassy in Warsaw gave me an opportunity to work with the diplomatic services. During my time there I learnt to promote the strengths of Sweden through public relations events, as part of a team. ___ / ___

5 My responsibilities included writing reports, organising official visits to Poland, and developing various internal and external projects. ___ / ___

6 The role of Public Relations Officer would allow me to develop my existing skills in an environment in which my political, linguistic and diplomatic skills could be utilised to their greatest potential. ___

Australian Embassy: Public Relations Officer

Department:	Department of Foreign Affairs and Trade
Immediate Supervisor:	First Secretary
Salary:	SEK 18,000 per month (Tax free)

DUTY STATEMENT:

a Monitor the Swedish, Finnish, Estonian, Latvian and Lithuanian media (including printed and electronic) each day; prepare a summary of key international and domestic news items.
b Monitor and prepare reports on international and domestic issues in Sweden, Finland, Estonia, Latvia and Lithuania.
c Organise programmes for visitors from Australia, and provide support to Australian-based staff in relation to high-level visits.
d Assist in the management and implementation of the Embassy's public affairs function and cultural affairs programme.

SELECTION CRITERIA AND SKILLS REQUIRED:

e Bilingual Swedish/English language and translation skills – both written and spoken
f High-level understanding of Swedish government, economy, business and EU processes
g Ability to prioritise, manage time effectively and work both independently and as part of a team
h Personal contacts in the media (desirable)
i Experience in a public relations and/or a media-related field (desirable)

Please note that to be considered, applicants must address the selection criteria when making their applications and all applications must be in English.

f Underline useful phrases from Hanna's letter which you could use in your own cover letter. For example, *I am confident that the combination of my* … *and* … *makes me an ideal candidate for the position*.

g Complete the following sentences using the phrases in the box from Hanna's letter.

> As a result   As part of my   During my period of employment at   During my time having   In the course of my current job   Since I work with   where I gained
> ~~While I was a~~

1 _____*While I was a*_____ team leader at Global Computers, I introduced new quality control procedures resulting in a 50% fall in customer complaints.

2 _____ at Legal Solutions, I was responsible for marketing software services.

3 _____ degree course in Business Studies, I worked for three months in the Data Processing department of a large computer corporation, _____ experience in IT solutions.

4 _____ Star Enterprises I gained some knowledge of accounting, _____ assisted their bookkeeper for three months.

5 _____ I have been responsible for the organisation of conferences. _____ my knowledge and experience in this field have grown considerably and I now feel capable of managing events independently.

6 _____ people every day in a business setting, I have developed strong interpersonal and communicative skills.

h Complete the following sentences so they are true for you.

1 While I was _____ I was in charge of _____

2 During _____ I was responsible for _____

3 As part of my degree course in _____ at _____
_____ I _____

4 During my period of employment at _____ I gained
_____

5 At present I am responsible for _____ . As a result _____
_____

6 Since I _____
_____

i In pairs, discuss your recent work experience, or time at university. Highlight the skills you feel you have developed through these experiences. What are the main skills you have that make you more employable?

Writing an effective final paragraph

The final paragraph of your cover letter should round the letter off, leaving the
reader with a positive impression of your application and a desire to interview you.

5 a **In pairs, decide whether the following statements are True (T) or False (F).**

1 The final paragraph should express willingness to provide any further
information that the reader may want. ___

2 It is not necessary to mention any items (including the CV) you are enclosing/
attaching. ___

3 It is polite to thank the reader for their time and consideration. ___

4 The final paragraph may actually consist of two short paragraphs. ___

b **Look back at the cover letters on pages 35 and 39. Did Jane and Hanna
follow this advice?**

c **Read the following paragraphs taken from British and American cover letters.
What differences in style do you notice?**

1 I look forward to hearing from you in the near future to schedule an interview at
a time convenient to you. During the interview I hope to learn more about your
company's plans and goals and discuss how I might contribute to the success of the
service team.

Sincere regards,

2 Should you have any queries regarding my application, or require any further information,
please do not hesitate to contact me. I would like to thank you in advance for your time and
consideration.

I look forward to hearing from you.

Yours faithfully,

3 I know that CVs help you to sort out the probables from the possibles, but they are no way to
judge the personal calibre of an individual. I would like to meet you and demonstrate that along
with the credentials, I have the personality that makes for a successful team player.

Yours truly,

4 You will find enclosed a copy of my curriculum vitae, which gives further details of my
education and my career to date. I would welcome the opportunity to discuss my professional
history and qualifications with you in greater detail.

Thank you in advance for your consideration.

Yours sincerely,

d **In pairs, discuss the following questions.**

1 Which extracts most closely follow the advice in Exercise 5a?

2 Which approach do you prefer and why?

3 Which approach would be most suitable for the country you are applying for
work in?

4 What, if anything, would you need to change if you wanted to use one of these
paragraphs in your own cover letter?

e Read the following final paragraphs. What do you think is good or bad about them?

1

> My experience and other technical skills are too extensive to be listed here. I would appreciate the opportunity to meet with you to discuss my credentials at your earliest convenience.
> I look forward to hearing from you.

2

> I would welcome the opportunity to discuss with you how I might contribute to your company in fulfilling its present goals. I will be available for appointment from 1st July.
> Thank you in advance for your consideration.

f ▶3.4 Listen to recruitment consultants, Grace and Oliver, discussing the extracts in Exercise 5e. What advice do they give? Do you agree with their comments?

g Think of a specific job you would like to apply for. Write your own closing paragraph using the phrases in the box and ideas from this section.

> I look forward to hearing from you.
> I would welcome/appreciate the opportunity to ...
> Please do not hesitate to contact me.
> should you have/require ...
> Thank you in advance for your time and consideration.

Using appropriate language

Whether applying online or sending your cover letter through the post, it is important to write using appropriate language. Although informal language may sometimes be acceptable in cover letters, more formal alternatives will create a more professional impression.

6 a Complete the following table using the words in the box.

> about   additional   contact   employer   employment   ensure   give
> looking   more   ~~receive~~   request   require   show   talk about   tell   want

Informal		Formal
get	→	1 *receive*
extra	→	2 _____
3 _____	→	would like
need	→	4 _____
5 _____	→	discuss
get in touch with	→	6 _____
7 _____	→	concerning/regarding
make sure	→	8 _____
9 _____	→	provide somebody with
10 _____	→	inform
boss	→	11 _____
12 _____	→	further/greater
13 _____	→	searching
ask for	→	14 _____
work/job	→	15 _____
16 _____	→	demonstrate

b Complete the following sentences using the formal words in Exercise 6a. In sentences 4 and 5, why is *should* used instead of *if*?

1 I am writing in response to our telephone conversation on 9ᵗʰ May <u>regarding</u> the secretarial vacancy.

2 I have recently graduated with a Master's degree in computing and am currently _____ for suitable _____ in the electronics field.

3 I would appreciate the opportunity to meet you, where I could _____ my skills, capabilities and professional experience in _____ detail.

4 I would be happy to _____ you _____ further references should you require them.

5 Should you _____ any _____ information _____ my application, please do not hesitate to _____ me.

c Rewrite the underlined sections of the following sentences using more appropriate formal language. Try to use the word in brackets.

1 I am writing <u>about your ad</u> for a Business Development Manager in *The Economist*. (response) <u>in response to your advertisement</u>

2 I am writing <u>to ask if you've got any vacancies at the moment</u> in your human resources department. (currently) _____

3 I am writing to apply for <u>the financial administrator job</u>. (position) _____

4 As you will see from my CV, my experience and qualifications <u>are what you're looking for</u>. (requirements) _____

5 The manager of your Milan Branch <u>told me to get in touch with you about</u> the opening for a media consultant. (recommended) _____

6 <u>Here's</u> a copy of my CV, and I look forward to an opportunity to demonstrate how my professional experience and skills would benefit Star Electronics. (attach) _____

7 <u>If you need any more info about</u> my application, please do not hesitate to contact me. (should) _____

8 <u>Thanks</u> for your time and consideration. (would) _____

d The following extract from a cover letter is too informal. Rewrite the extract using appropriate formal language.

> Dear Sarah,
>
> I saw your advert for a job as a secretary on the Internet last week. I want to apply for the job.
>
> I've been working as a secretary at Gordon's Financial Services in Barcelona for the last three years, but I'm looking for a new job in Milan because my husband has just got a new job with his company in Milan.
>
> I've heard a lot about your company. I think it's one of the biggest financial service companies in Milan. I've worked for years in this area (over six years) and think that this has given me the experience that your company needs.
>
> If you want to meet to talk about how my skills and experience can benefit your company in the future, I would be happy to come in and meet you.
>
> Kind regards, Jane

Dear Ms Mattin,

_____

_____

_____

_____

_____

_____

_____

_____

_____

Writing a cover letter

7 a Look at the example of a bad cover letter that Felix sent Vicky. In pairs, discuss the mistakes he has labelled (a–o).

Baldrick College
Swinton
SW4 8BT
Nat1987@bcs.ac.uk
PrincessNL@gmail.com **a**

14 October 2008

Ace Consultants
45 Strand
London WC2 8LK

b Dear Sir or Madam, **c**

I would like to apply for a job at your company when I graduate this **d**
summer.

f I have always wanted to work with a strategic management
consultancy firm which helps it's clients make lasting and **e**
substantial improvements, and I cannot imagine a better place to
work than Hillier and Thomson. **g**

I am extremely confident that my university course has prepared
me for a career in management. Whilst at university I had a number
h of part-time jobs and I would say that my main strength is my
ability to get on with other people. I am a very sociable person and
i through a range of social activities I have perffected my outstanding
communication skills. **j**
k

As you will see from my CV I am not familiar with many computer
programmes, but I would like to learn and am sure that I would pick
l things up quickly. I really want a job which will give me the chance
to travel, as this is a particular interest of mine.
m

I would be truly grateful to be invited for an interview and to be
n given a chance to further discuss my application.

Yours,

Natalie Laurent

o

b Match Felix's advice (1–15) to the appropriate parts of the cover letter (a–o) in Exercise 7a.

1   Find a named person to write to. _b_
2   Make your letter specific to each company you write to and make it clear what job you're applying for. ___
3   Don't copy phrases from websites and brochures. Use your own words. ___
4   Make sure the name of the company matches the one in the address. ___
5   Research and be clear about the job you are applying for. Strategic management consulting is not the same as management. ___
6   Mistakes of spelling and grammar are unacceptable – always double-check. ___
7   Make it clear what you bring to the organisation, not just what you can gain. ___
8   Don't apologise for skills you haven't got, especially where they are not a strict requirement of the job. ___
9   Don't exaggerate your level of skill. Always use examples to substantiate what you say. ___
10 End your letter '*Yours sincerely*' (if to a named person) or '*Yours faithfully*' (if not). ___
11 Be polite and respectful but not excessively so. ___
12 Don't be vague about your aptitudes. Make sure you know what the recruiter is looking for and then provide specific evidence, highlighting key parts of your CV. ___
13 Don't start all/most paragraphs with '*I*'. ___
14 Use apostrophes correctly (here *its* not *it's*). ___
15 Just give one email address (keep this plain and sensible). ___

c Rewrite the cover letter in Exercise 7a, using the language and advice from this unit. Then compare your letter with the model letter on page 111.

d Research a real job that you would be interested in applying for. Spend some time researching the company and the position in more depth. Think about the skills and experience that you have that are relevant for the post and then write a cover letter for the job.

UNIT 4 Successful interviews

- Preparing for the interview
- Making a positive first impression
- Dealing effectively with interview questions
- Talking about yourself
- Avoiding common mistakes
- Proving you've done your research
- Demonstrating you've got what it takes

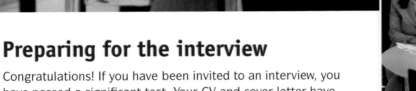

Preparing for the interview

Congratulations! If you have been invited to an interview, you have passed a significant test. Your CV and cover letter have made a strong first impression. You have been selected in front of your rivals, and made it to the short list.

Preparation is the key to a successful interview. The other candidates may have similar qualifications, skills and experience. The interview is your opportunity to prove you are the best candidate for the job. Ensuring you are well-prepared will help you to reduce stress, increase your confidence and improve your chances of being offered the job.

1 a In pairs, discuss the following questions.

1 Have you ever been interviewed for a job in English? How did it go?
2 How do you feel about going for an interview?
3 How can you prepare for an interview?

b In pairs, discuss the following tips for preparing for an interview. Which ones do you think are more important? Which ones would you do first?

- Try to predict the questions you are likely to be asked during the interview.
- Do some research into the company you are applying for a job with.
- Find out exactly what the job involves.
- Analyse your skills and experience and identify areas where they match the job requirements and the company needs.
- Rehearse the interview.
- Decide what you're going to wear.
- Prepare a list of questions to ask at the end of the interview.

Making a positive first impression

Before you arrive

You never get a second chance to make a first impression. People start forming their impression of you immediately, looking at the outside and making assumptions about the inside. It is your responsibility to ensure that you send out the right message about who you are, through your physical appearance, your clothes and your body language.

2 a Imagine you met somebody new today. After a few minutes talking to you, what might they say about you, for example how successful or wealthy you are, your level of education, or your professionalism?

b In pairs, discuss what you can do to create a positive first impression with an interviewer. Think about the following points.

- your appearance
- body language
- how to 'break the ice' with the interviewer

c In pairs, discuss the following interview tips. Write *do* or *don't* next to each tip.

1 Arrive ten minutes early.
2 Speak English with a friend before the interview.
3 Bring a close friend or relative with you for support.
4 Take a copy of your CV and examples of your work with you.
5 Learn some impressive words and phrases to use in the interview.
6 Memorise long answers to questions that you anticipate being asked.

d ▶4.1 Silvia Carnali has been invited for an interview at the communications agency, Futerra. Before her interview she meets Nina, a human resources manager, for some interview preparation tips. Listen to the conversation and write Nina's opinion (*do/don't*) next to the tips (1–6) in Exercise 2c. Do you agree with Nina? What tips does Nina mention that are not included in the list above?

Small talk

The outcome of an interview can be decided in the first five minutes. From the moment you arrive for an interview you are being assessed. Even before the interview itself begins you will be communicating a message about who you are. In order to create a positive impression, it's important that from the moment you arrive what you say is clear, confident and enthusiastic.

3 a ▶4.2 Listen to extracts from the beginning of Silvia's interview at Futerra and Alex Mencken's interview at a London theatre. Answer the following questions.

1 Why is Mr Lewis late for the interview?
2 What does Silvia read while she's waiting?
3 What useful information does Silvia get from the receptionist?
4 How does Silvia create a positive first impression with Mr Lewis?
5 What do Alex and Karl chat about before the interview?
6 How does Alex create a positive first impression with Karl?

b In pairs, discuss the following questions.

1 Silvia is very polite to the receptionist. Why is this important?
2 What does Silvia ask the receptionist? How could this help her application?
3 Alex mentions that a friend of his who works at the theatre suggested he applied for the job. Do you think this was a good idea?

c ▶4.2 Match the conversation openings (1–8) to the responses (a–h). Listen to the extracts again and check your answers.

1	I'm afraid Mr Lewis is in a meeting at the moment.	a	No, no trouble at all.
2	Can I get you anything while you wait?	b	No, thank you, I'm fine.
3	I'm sorry I'm late. Our meeting overran a bit.	c	I know. It's awful, isn't it?
		d	Thank you. It's nice to meet you too.
4	How are you?	e	You were highly recommended to me by a friend.
5	It's nice to meet you at last.	f	I'm very well, thank you.
6	Did you have any trouble finding us?	g	That's quite all right.
7	I can't believe the weather at the moment!	h	That's okay. I was just admiring the office.
8	How did you find out about us?		

d In pairs, practise the small talk in Exercise 3c.

e Look at the following examples of interview small talk. Match the beginnings (1–10) to the endings (a–j). Would you say these to the receptionist (R), the interviewer (I) or both (B)?

1	Do you think I could have	a	I got caught in the rain. ____
2	Do you have a company brochure	b	your toilet to freshen up? ____
3	I'm very sorry I'm late.	c	a glass of water while I'm waiting? _R_
4	Do you think I could use	d	I was planning to be here over an hour ago, but my train was cancelled. ____
5	I was just admiring your office.	e	I could have a look at while I'm waiting? ____
6	Are there many other candidates	f	Is it always this busy? ____
7	I had terrible problems parking here.	g	It all looks very modern. Is it new? ____
8	I'm afraid I'm not feeling very well.	h	Do you have many people working elsewhere? ____
9	The office is smaller than I expected.	i	Could I sit down for a few minutes? ____
10	Is there somewhere I could leave my umbrella?	j	scheduled for interviews today? ____

f Having some small talk helps to build a positive rapport with the interviewer. In the UK the weather and transport problems are very common and appropriate small talk topics. In pairs, discuss the following questions.

1 What small talk topics are commonly discussed in your country?
2 Are there any things you would avoid talking about?

g In pairs, role play arriving at an interview and making small talk with the receptionist.

Student A, you are the candidate. Try to get some useful information from the receptionist which you can use later in your interview.

Student B, you are the receptionist.

Swap roles and practise again.

Body language

Much of the impact you create at an interview is based on your body language, and getting this right is essential. The way you walk, sit and act may influence your interviewer's opinion of you as much as what you actually say.

4 a In pairs, discuss the following questions.

1 How could your body language let you down in an interview?
2 How can you avoid these problems?

b ▶4.3 Listen to five people speaking about body language and bad first impressions in interviews. Write the extract number (1–5) next to the problem it mentions. Then match each problem (a–e) to the advice on how to avoid it (A–E).

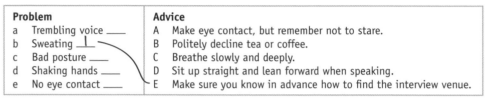

Problem	Advice
a Trembling voice ____	A Make eye contact, but remember not to stare.
b Sweating __1__	B Politely decline tea or coffee.
c Bad posture ____	C Breathe slowly and deeply.
d Shaking hands ____	D Sit up straight and lean forward when speaking.
e No eye contact ____	E Make sure you know in advance how to find the interview venue.

c What tips on body language would you give someone being interviewed for a job in your country?

Dealing effectively with interview questions

Responding to questions at an interview is your opportunity to give evidence of your skills and experience, prove you know what the job entails, and demonstrate that you are the best person for the job.

5 a In pairs, discuss the following questions.

1 What questions might you expect to be asked in any job interview?
2 What advice would you give somebody about dealing with interview questions?

b Look at the following common interview questions. Write the type of question (a–c) next to each question (1–12).

a Questions that require you to talk about yourself, your ambitions, your personality, your hobbies and interests
b Questions that require you to prove you have researched the job and company you have applied for work with
c Questions that require you to demonstrate you have the skills and experience required for the job

1 Can you tell us something about yourself? _a_
2 What experience do you have that is relevant for this position? ____
3 What did you learn during your time at university? ____
4 What do you see as your strengths? ____
5 What do you think about our website? ____
6 What attracted you to the position? ____
7 How would your colleagues describe you? ____
8 What sorts of projects did you work on in your last position? ____
9 What university did you attend and why did you choose it? ____
10 How do you typically approach new projects? ____ ____
11 What do you know about our company? ____
12 Where do you see yourself in five years' time? ____

c In pairs, try to think of some more questions for each category (a–c). Which questions would you welcome in an interview? Which questions would you not like to be asked?

d In pairs, take turns to ask and answer the questions in Exercises 5b and 5c. Which questions are easiest to answer? Which are the most difficult?

e ▶4.4 Listen to three extracts from an interview. Which three questions in Exercise 5b is the candidate responding to?

f ▶4.4 Listen again and, in pairs, discuss how each answer could be improved.

g Match the advice on how to answer questions (1–5) to the practical tips (a–e). What were the specific problems with the three extracts in Exercise 5e?

1	Be clear and explicit	a	If you personally did something, say 'I did' rather than 'we did' or 'it was'.
		b	Most lies or exaggerations get discovered and suggest bad judgment on your part.
2	Be audible	c	Do not assume interviewers know what your previous job involved, even if they work in the same organisation. It is also important not to use jargon or acronyms that the interviewer might not be familiar with.
3	Be concise		
		d	Don't talk for too long, or drift away from the point. Be alert to any signs from the interviewer of boredom, loss of concentration, or signals that you are talking too much. However, also ensure that you say enough.
4	Be truthful		
5	Focus on action you have taken	e	Answers that can't be heard demonstrate poor interpersonal and communicative skills.

h Look at the first interview extract from Exercise 5e. Rewrite the candidate's answer and improve it by:
- deleting any sections which drift away from the point;
- trying to make the remaining sentences more dynamic.

Well, I've never really thought about it. I suppose I'd like to be married with kids, perhaps. My sister's got three kids, and they're really great. I'd also like to be doing a job I enjoy. There's nothing worse than being stuck in a boring job where you have the same routine every day. It'd be a job with lots of responsibility, but I suppose not too much. I wouldn't want to get stressed. If I was lucky enough to get this job, it'd be great, but I suppose five years is a long time without a change, so I'd try to get a promotion, if I could.

I see myself doing a job I really enjoy.

_____

_____

_____

_____

i ▶4.5 Listen to an improved answer and compare it with your ideas. What techniques did the candidate use in the improved answer?

j Look at the third interview extract from Exercise 5e. Rewrite the candidate's answer and improve it by:

- trying to make it more action-focused – make every sentence focus on what the speaker actually does or did;
- adding specific examples.

Well, usually there needs to be a clear picture of what the aims of the project are. So it's essential to speak to everyone involved before taking any action. In my current job we use project management software to help us keep track of what we have to do and when we have to do it. Of course, it's important that someone keeps an eye on whether people are actually doing what they're supposed to be doing, and obviously you also need to deal with unexpected situations as they come up.

The first thing I do is make sure I've got a really clear picture of what I
need to achieve. Let me give you an example ...
_____
_____
_____
_____
_____

k ▶4.6 Listen to an improved answer and compare it with your ideas.

l In pairs, take turns to ask and answer the three questions in Exercise 5e.

Talking about yourself

In all interviews you will be required to talk about yourself. The interviewers want to find out whether you're the type of person who would be able to do the job and also whether your personality would fit in with the rest of the company.

6 a In pairs, discuss how you would answer the following questions.

1 Can you tell us something about yourself?
2 What did you learn during your time at university?
3 What kinds of things do you worry about?
4 Would you say you're an ambitious person?

b ▶4.7 Alejandro is a recent Economics graduate, practising for an interview at an international bank. Listen to his answers to the four questions in Exercise 6a. In pairs, discuss what you think of Alejandro's answers, and suggest ways in which he could improve them.

c ▶4.8 Listen to a recruitment expert, Grace, commenting on each of Alejandro's answers. Do you agree with her?

d ▶4.9 Listen to the answers Alejandro gives in the real interview. How has he improved his responses?

e ▶4.9 **Complete Alejandro's improved answers using the correct form of the verbs in the box. Listen again and check your answers.**

apply	communicate	develop	gain	get (x2)
lead	make	meet	motivate	~~put~~ work

Interviewer: *Can you tell us something about yourself?*

Alejandro: *Well, I'm motivated and I* (1) __put__ *a lot of effort into everything I do, whether I'm studying at university, at work or even when I'm playing sport. During my last year at university I was captain of the basketball team. I had to organise matches and* (2) _____ *the players. As captain it was essential that I was able to* (3) _____ *effectively and get along with everybody in the team ... and for the first time in years our team managed to reach the regional final. We didn't win, unfortunately, but* (4) _____ *the team to the final was a big achievement for me.*

Interviewer: *What did you learn during your time at university?*

Alejandro: *Oh, lots of things. My Economics degree was very practical, and there were many elements of the degree that could be* (5) _____ *to the business world. I had a number of challenging assignments, which often had to be completed within a short period of time. This helped me to* (6) _____ *my prioritising skills and ability to* (7) _____ *to tight deadlines.*

Interviewer: *What kinds of things do you worry about?*

Alejandro: *I worry about normal things, the same as everybody else, I think. I worry about* (8) _____ *deadlines and* (9) _____ *everything done on time. I used to worry about data on my computer quite a bit. Now I back up all my data on an external hard drive, so that everything is protected. This way I've got one less thing to worry about.*

Interviewer: *Would you say you're an ambitious person?*

Alejandro: *Yes, I would say that I'm ambitious. I'm very keen to* (10) _____ *a job with a company such as yours where I can* (11) _____ *full use of my degree and professional experience. I am a dedicated worker and would hope to* (12) _____ *internal promotion based on my performance at work.*

f **Underline useful phrases from Alejandro's answers in Exercise 6e which you could use to answer the same questions. For example, *I put a lot of effort into everything I do, whether I'm* ... *or even when I'm* ... Plan your own answers to the questions.**

g **In pairs, take turns to ask and answer the questions.**

Avoiding common mistakes

Whatever job you're applying for, there are some questions that you will nearly always get asked. Preparing for these questions will help you to use them to demonstrate effectively why you are the best candidate for the position.

7 a **In pairs, discuss how you would answer the following questions. Then, take turns to ask and answer them.**

1   What do you see as your strengths?
2   What university did you attend, and why did you choose it?
3   What are your weaknesses?
4   What do you like doing in your spare time?

b ►4.10 Listen to two recruitment experts, Grace and Oliver, sharing tips on effective ways to answer these questions. Do you agree with them? What would you change about your own answers to make them more effective?

c ►4.10 Match the advice given by Grace and Oliver (a–h) to the questions (1–4) in Exercise 7a. Listen again and check your answers.

a   Use examples from your experience to support your claims. ⊥

b   Don't say that you chose it because it was the closest one to home. ___

c   Mention what steps you have taken to tackle this problem. ___

d   Focus on the educational/academic/professional reasons for your choice. ___

e   Don't use tentative language such as 'I feel' or 'I think I'm quite good at'. ___

f   Mention anything that demonstrates you working as part of a team or group. ___

g   Don't say that you have none. ___

h   Talk about things that are unusual and memorable. ___

d ►4.11 Lidia and Rafa are both applying for a marketing position with a magazine based in New York. Listen to their answers to the questions in Exercise 7a and decide who is the stronger candidate.

e ►4.11 Complete the following extracts from Lidia's interview. Listen again and check your answers.

1   *I'm also able to prioritise my work and work under* **pressure** *if deadlines are moved forward.*

2   *I did a lot of _____ into universities, both abroad and in Spain.*

3   *In the end I decided to go to the University of Barcelona as it was clear that its Economics department had an excellent _____ .*

4   *Well, my French is a bit rusty, so I have _____ started evening classes to improve it.*

5   *I still play _____ for a local club and love going away with the team for matches against other clubs.*

6   *I'm also a _____ traveller.*

7   *During the summer last year I _____ a month in Africa working with volunteers at a national reserve.*

f Look at the following answer templates based on Lidia's answers. Complete the templates so they are true for you.

1   I am _____ and apply a _____ approach to my work.
    I believe in _____ . This enables me to _____ . I'm also
    able to _____ . For example, in my last job _____ .
    I implemented a new system for _____ . This way we were able to
    _____ .

2   I did a lot of research into _____ . In the end I decided to
    _____ as it was clear that its _____ had an excellent
    reputation.

3   Well, I feel that _____ , so I have recently started _____
    to improve _____ . I used to be _____ , but I've started
    _____ , which has enabled me to _____ .

4   I enjoy _____ . I'm also a keen _____ . During the
    _____ I _____ . I'm currently _____ .

g In pairs, take turns to ask and answer the questions in Exercise 7a, using the templates in Exercise 7f.

Proving you've done your research

Successful candidates are the ones who research the job and the company. They are able to walk into an interview confident they have exactly what the company is looking for.

8 a ▶ **4.12 During her interview with Futerra, Silvia Carnali is asked what she knows about the company, and why she wants to work there. Listen to the extract from the interview and answer the following questions.**

1 What did Silvia do before applying for the position at Futerra?
2 What attracted Silvia to Futerra?
3 What experience will Silvia be able to use in the job?
4 What did Silvia like about Futerra's website?
5 Would Silvia prefer to work for a large or small organisation?

b ▶ **4.12 Complete the following extracts from Silvia's interview using the phrases in the box. Listen again and check your answers.**

attracted me to	dynamic place to work	from everything I've learnt
It's clear from	look at your website	~~research into the market~~
well-established reputation		

1 *Well, before applying for this position I did some* <u>research into the market</u> *and Futerra came out on top.*
2 *I had a* _____ *and could see that you work with a variety of people …*
3 *Well, it's really something that* _____ *Futerra.*
4 *The Junior Consultant post combines these two areas at a company with a* _____ .
5 *You came across online as an exciting,* _____ .
6 _____ *your website that Futerra is a quite a small company …*
7 *I definitely feel,* _____ *about Futerra, that this is the type of organisation I'd like to work for.*

c ▶ **4.13 Listen to the interviewers, Matt and Dan, discussing Silvia's performance in the interview. Do you agree with their comments?**

d When demonstrating that you've researched the company, you should mention positive things that attracted you to the company. Find examples of positive expressions in audioscript 4.12 on page 90. Can you think of any more examples of positive language of your own?

e Cross out the word in bold that cannot be used to complete each of the following sentences.

1 I had a look at your website. It's really **impressive/innovative/~~challenging~~/eye-catching**.
2 I wanted to work with this company because you have a really **strong/enjoyable/outstanding/excellent** reputation.
3 The work you do seems to be very **fulfilling/worthwhile/satisfying/first-class**.
4 I was impressed by your **fulfilling/innovative/first-class/best-selling** products.
5 I think working for you would be very **enjoyable/challenging/fantastic/fulfilling**.

f Think of a company you would like to work for. Plan your answers to the following questions. In pairs, role play the interview. Student A, you are the interviewer. Student B, you are the candidate. Swap roles and practise again.

- What do you know about _____ ? And why would you like to work here?
- Can tell us why this impressed you?
- Can you tell us a bit more about what attracted you to the position of _____ ?
- You mentioned that you looked at our website. What did you think of it?
- Wouldn't you prefer to work for a _____ organisation?

Demonstrating you've got what it takes

In every interview you will be asked to talk about your transferable skills and experience and how these meet the requirements for the job.

9 a ▶4.14 Susana Cilveti is a recent graduate. Listen to an extract from her interview for a sales assistant position and answer the following questions.

1 What skills does Susana think are necessary for a sales assistant?
2 What was she doing before she moved to England?
3 What evidence does she give of her financial experience?
4 Susana claims to be a highly effective communicator. Do you think she provides enough evidence to support this claim?

b ▶4.14 Listen again and complete the following sentences so they are true for Susana by underlining the correct words in bold.

1 In my last job I was responsible for **implementing new strategies** / <u>**selling souvenirs**</u> / **negotiating deals**.
2 I am used to **dealing with customers** / **managing big budgets** / **coping with problems**.
3 I can speak Italian **reasonably well** / **a little** / **fluently**.
4 This period of employment gave me experience of **managing people** / **networking** / **organising events**.
5 When I was at university I used to be **editor of the university magazine** / **a member of the student council** / **captain of the volleyball team**.
6 I feel I am a **well-organised person** / **highly effective communicator** / **reliable and efficient employee**.
7 I can work **well under pressure** / **well autonomously** / **best as part of a team**.
8 I am able to **be firm but fair** / **delegate effectively** / **use my initiative to solve problems**.

c Choose the best ending for each sentence in Exercise 9b so they are true for you. You can invent your own endings.

d In pairs, take turns to ask and answer the following questions, using your answers in Exercise 9c to help you.

1 What languages can you speak?
2 How would you describe the way you work?
3 What skills did you develop at university / at your last job?

e ▶4.15 In her interview at Futerra, Silvia Carnali is asked how her skills and experience match the requirements for the position. Listen to the extract and make a note of the skills she mentions.

f ▶4.15 Silvia uses a range of phrases to organise her answer. Complete her answer using the phrases in the box. Listen again and check your answers.

> also when   ever since   finally   Firstly   Following
> For example   For my dissertation   for three reasons
> ~~I think I'm suitable for the position at Futerra because~~
> Secondly   So   So to sum up   That's really when
> When I was at   years ago

Well, (1) _I think I'm suitable for the position at Futerra because_ *I understand the issues you deal with and am passionate about them. Four* (2) _____ *I joined Greenpeace and have been an active member* (3) _____ .

(4) _____ *my BA I found out about an exciting project in Kenya and spent six months there educating local people about the need for reforestation.* (5) _____ *I started getting interested in sustainability and* (6) _____ *I started learning about different communication strategies.* (7) _____ , *our team found that simply putting up posters didn't really have much of an impact, but going and talking to respected members of the community and getting them to talk to others was much more effective.*

(8) _____ *university I was the communications officer of the student union and I was responsible for dealing with suppliers and other student organisations.* (9) _____ *I've got quite a lot of communication experience. I know you're also looking for someone who's good at research.* (10) _____ *for my MA I'm researching how best to communicate reforestation issues, building on my own practical experiences gained in Kenya.*

(11) _____ , *I think I'm suitable for the position at Futerra* (12) _____ . (13) _____ , *I've done a lot of communication work.* (14) _____ , *I'm a good team worker, and* (15) _____ , *because I have a good understanding of the sustainability issues this agency deals with.*

g Underline useful phrases from Silvia's answer which you could use in an interview of your own. For example, *I think I'm suitable for the position at* … *because I* …

h Put the following stages in the same order as Silvia's answer.
1 Talking about your experience, providing background information for an anecdote
2 Summarising how the various examples have fully answered the question
3 Giving specific details from previous experiences and showing how these experiences relate to the requirements of the job
4 Expressing enthusiasm for the job and briefly relating your character to the job
5 Giving a second example of experience that relates to the job requirements

i Think of a job that you would like to apply for. Plan your answer to the question, '*How do your skills and experience match the requirements for this position?*' using the structure in Exercise 9h.

j Complete the following sentences so they are true for you.

1 I think I'm suitable for the position of _____ , because _____ _____ .

2 Following my degree I _____ .

3 I started getting interested in _____ .

4 When I was at university I _____ .

5 So to sum up, I think I'm suitable for the position at _____ for three reasons. Firstly, _____ . Secondly, _____ , and finally _____ .

k Look at the following table and add two more common interview questions. Think of a job you would like to apply for. Prepare your answers to all the questions using words and phrases from this unit.

Question	Clear	Explicit	Audible	Concise	Truthful	Action language	Body language
Can you tell us something about yourself?							
What do you see as your strengths?							
What do you like doing in your spare time?							
What do you know about our company?							
How do your skills and experience match the requirements for this position?							

l In groups of three role play a job interview using the table in Exercise 9k.

Student A, you are the interviewer. You should ask a selection of questions from the table in Exercise 9k.

Student B, you are the candidate. You should answer the questions honestly, using your notes in Exercise 9k.

Student C, you are the observer. You should make notes on the candidate's answers in the table in Exercise 9k, using ✓ and ✗ symbols.

If possible, record the interview, as this will help you to identify your individual strengths and weaknesses. When you have finished, the observer should give feedback on the candidate's performance. Swap roles and practise again.

UNIT 5

Advanced interview techniques

- Handling competency-based questions
- Demonstrating your skills
- Talking about your weaknesses
- Asking questions of your own
- Dealing with telephone interviews

Handling competency-based questions

Competencies are a combination of knowledge, skills and behaviour required to do a specific job.

1 a **In pairs, ask and answer one of the following interview questions.**

1 Tell me about a time when you had to make a difficult decision.
2 Tell me about a time when you demonstrated good customer service.
3 Tell me about a time when you showed strong leadership skills.
4 Tell me about a time when you played an important role in a team.
5 Tell me about a time when you experienced pressure at university or at work.

b ▶5.1 **Listen to three people each answering one of the questions in Exercise 1a successfully. Identify which question each speaker is answering.**

Speaker 1 ___   Speaker 2 ___   Speaker 3 ___

c **In pairs, discuss how you think each story ends. What would be an impressive conclusion to each story, to really demonstrate that the speaker possesses the necessary competency?**

d ▶5.2 **Now listen to the rest of the extracts to check your predictions in Exercise 1c. Were your ideas similar?**

e **The questions in Exercise 1a are all examples of competency-based questions. In pairs, discuss the following questions.**

1 What is an interviewer looking for in competency-based questions?
2 Why is it essential to prepare stories before your interview?
3 How common are competency-based interview questions?

f ▶5.3 **Listen to two recruitment experts, Grace and Oliver, discussing competency-based questions and compare their ideas with your answers in Exercise 1e.**

g A common technique for planning and structuring answers to competency-based questions is the STAR method. Look at the diagram below. What do you think the initials S, T, A and R stand for?

S___
Set the scene and give the context. Give an outline of a specific real situation or problem that you faced in the past

T___
Go into more detail and identify the specific aspects you focused on and why. What was the target or task necessary to improve the situation?

A___
Describe the specific action that you took in order to improve the situation. What did you do, how did you do it, when did you do it and why did you do it?

R___
Finish by talking about the outcomes of your action and the difference it made. What happened in the end, what was accomplished, and what did you learn?

h ▶ 5.2 Listen to the extracts in Exercise 1d again. For each story, identify the four sections (S, T, A and R).

i Look at the sentences from the candidates' stories and answer the following questions.

1 Which phrasal verb is used to describe an unexpected success?
2 Which phrasal verb is used to introduce an unexpected cause?
3 Which phrasal verb is used to introduce an unexpected result?

*It **turned out** that his accountant had been taken ill …*

*So we actually **ended up** getting paid within a week …*

*So it all **worked out** in the end.*

j Prepare a STAR diagram for one of the questions in Exercise 1a. Try to use the three phrasal verbs in Exercise 1i.

Demonstrating your skills

It is essential you provide evidence of how you acted in real situations in the past in order to show you have the transferable skills required for the job you are applying for.

2 a ▶ 5.4 After applying for a variety of positions at leading international pharmaceutical companies, Communications Manager Vicky Tang is invited to attend an interview at Clyde & Johnson's. Listen to an extract from her interview and answer the following questions.

1 Where is Vicky from?
2 Where did she go to university?

b ▶ 5.5 Listen to another candidate for the same position, Pieter Volker, responding to the same question, and answer the following questions.

1 Where did Pieter do his first degree?
2 What did he do at the University of St Petersburg?
3 Where did he spend his student work placement?

c In pairs, discuss Vicky's and Pieter's techniques for tackling the question about their educational background. Whose technique is more successful?

d ▶5.5 Listen to Pieter's answer again. Which of the following competencies does he demonstrate or suggest?

- customer service skills
- teamworking
- goal orientation
- flexibility
- leadership
- communication skills
- organisational skills
- decision-making skills
- interpersonal skills

e In pairs, talk about your educational experience. Try to demonstrate or suggest several of the competencies in Exercise 2d. Try to guess what competencies your partner is focusing on.

f ▶5.6 Listen to another extract from Vicky's interview and answer the following questions.

1 What problem did Green Pharmaceuticals have?
2 What did Vicky do to tackle this problem?
3 What was the effect of Vicky's actions?

g Vicky uses the STAR method to structure her answer. Underline phrases in her response that describe the four sections.

1 Situation (the problem Green Pharmaceuticals was facing)
2 Target (the solution to this problem)
3 Action (what Vicky did to solve the problem)
4 Result (the results of her actions)

At the moment I spend a lot of time travelling between Asia and Europe working with regional teams organising educational events, so I use both of these skills on a regular basis. Let me give you an example. As you know, the Chinese market is growing in all areas, including pharmaceuticals. However, at the time, Green Pharmaceuticals felt they didn't have enough contacts in China. It was clear that the situation wasn't very good for us. We needed to improve things. So in order to increase our number of contacts in China I decided to organise a pharmaceutical conference in Beijing. It was my responsibility to ensure that all the right people were invited. I really had to use all my skills at communicating, in both English and Mandarin, to persuade people to participate. In the end my hard work resulted in a successful conference, with our employees meeting and talking to the right people. As a matter of fact this conference was such a success that it is now an annual event, and has led directly to closer professional relationships between Green Pharmaceuticals and key contacts in China.

h Add one phrase from Vicky's answer in Exercise 2g to each column in the following table.

Situation	Target	Action	Result
there was a time when ...	what needed to be done was ...	therefore I ...	this resulted in ...
I discovered that ...	it was very important that ...	I organised ...	this led to ...

i Add the phrases in the box to the table in Exercise 2h.

I agreed to ...   I wanted to be a bit more ...   probably the best example is ...
so I ...   So it all worked out in the end.   the problem was ...
there was one time when ...   we actually ended up ...

j In pairs, take turns to ask and answer the following common competency-based question, '*Tell me about a time when you had to resolve a difficult situation.*'

k ▶5.7 Listen to Vicky's response to the question in Exercise 2j. In pairs, discuss the following questions.

1 What was the problem?
2 What did Vicky do to solve the problem?
3 What skills did Vicky use to solve the problem?
4 Would you have handled the situation in the same way?

l ▶5.7 Vicky uses a range of expressions to structure her answer. Complete her answer using the phrases in the box. Listen again and check your answers.

> Anyway, what happened was   As soon as   I managed to
> I then   In the end   It was very important
> So I decided to   ~~There was a time when~~
> Unfortunately this meant that   which I'd organised beforehand

Okay. (1) __There was a time when__ I was organising a conference here in London. It was a couple of months ago, and it was a really important conference. (2) _____ one of the main guest speakers, who was due to give the opening address, had his flight cancelled and wasn't sure if he was going to make it on time. (3) _____ the participants were happy with the conference, and I knew they would be disappointed if he didn't show up. (4) _____ try and find another flight for the speaker. After a bit of negotiating with a different airline, (5) _____ get him booked onto a slightly later flight. (6) _____ even if he came straight from the airport, he would still be a bit late for the opening address. I took a risk and hoped that he wasn't going to be delayed any more. (7) _____ he'd landed I contacted him, and when I knew he was in a taxi and on his way, which was about five minutes before he was supposed to be on stage, I got up on the stage. (8) _____ told the participants about the situation and I invited them to have some coffee and cakes while we waited, (9) _____. Actually, they liked this, as it was a chance to network a little and get to know some of the other conference participants. When the speaker did finally arrive, it was actually difficult to get everybody back in the main hall. (10) _____ I managed to keep everybody happy and ensure that the conference went as smoothly as possible.

m Which tense does Vicky mainly use to give the key events of her story?

n In pairs, discuss what makes the following sentence from Vicky's answer memorable.

When the speaker did finally arrive, it was actually difficult to get everybody back in the main hall.

o Interview anecdotes are more likely to be interesting and memorable if they include some surprising information. In Vicky's anecdote in Exercise 2l she introduces a surprising fact with the word *actually*. You can also use *in fact* or *as a matter of fact*. Make the following sentences more memorable using *in fact*, *actually* or *as a matter of fact*. Several answers are possible.

1   My boss wasn't convinced that it was worth investing in India. However, my research managed to prove that it was.
2   As a result of my actions, what could have been a disaster turned out to be a big success.
3   My work had really helped, and I thought that I would be invited to join the marketing team permanently, but I was invited to lead the team!
4   I believed my suggestions would lead to bigger profits. What I didn't expect was that profits at the company would grow by nearly 20%!

p In pairs, take turns to ask and answer one of the questions in Exercise 1a on page 59. Use the STAR diagram you prepared in Exercise 1j and expressions from this section to structure your answers. Try to make your anecdotes surprising and memorable.

Talking about your weaknesses

Turning negatives into positives

In an interview you will almost certainly face challenging questions which attempt to assess your suitability for the job. It is vital to avoid getting caught in the trap of saying negative things about yourself. Preparing for these 'difficult' questions will help you keep your answers positive.

3 a ▶5.8 A recent graduate, Jarek, has been invited for an interview with an international financial company. He arranges to meet up with his friend, Olivia, who has been working there for a couple of years. Listen to their conversation and answer the following questions.

1   Who is going to interview Jarek?
2   Why did Jarek quit his last job?
3   What general advice does Olivia give Jarek?

b Compare Jarek's and Olivia's answers to the question, '*Why did you leave your last job?*' Complete Olivia's answer using the words in the box.

| although | develop | feel | further | liked | position |
| stretched | working | | | | |

Jarek's answer:

I hated my last job, I couldn't stand the boss. He used to drive me crazy! ... I handed in my notice and left as soon as I could.

Olivia's answer:

(1) Although I really (2) _____ my job, and the people I was (3) _____ with, I didn't (4) _____ I was being (5) _____ enough. I'm looking for a (6) _____ in which I can (7) _____ my professional skills (8) _____ .

c In pairs, discuss how you would answer the following questions.

1   What are your weaknesses?
2   Tell me about something you have found difficult at work.

d In pairs, try to complete the following advice with a suitable word. Do you agree with the advice?

1 In response to open questions you should never actively volunteer _____ information during an interview.
2 Employers like to ask you to give negative information not to _____ you, but to see what sort of person you are.
3 You will seem much more employable if you can show yourself as someone who sees problems as _____ .
4 Questions about weaknesses are actually a chance to demonstrate how you tackle and overcome _____ , and why you are the right person for the job.

e ▶5.9 **Listen to three different candidates responding to a question about their weaknesses. Match the candidates (1–3) to the techniques they use for tackling this question (a–c). Which answer did you like the most? Why?**

a Talk about a character flaw that could ultimately be viewed as a positive characteristic.
b Talk about something that is no longer a weakness. Mention how you overcame the weakness and that you have solved similar problems more recently.
c Talk about a knowledge-based weakness, which is easily overcome. Mention why this weakness isn't a serious problem and what steps you are actively taking to solve the problem.

Candidate 1 ____
Candidate 2 ____
Candidate 3 ____

f In pairs, discuss the advantages of each technique.

g Which of the three candidates in Exercise 3e used the STAR technique to answer this question?

Softening and emphasis

When answering interview questions that require negative information you should soften any negatives in your response and emphasise any positive information.

4 a Look at the first candidate's response from Exercise 3e. In pairs, discuss why the candidate doesn't simply say, '*In the past I used to procrastinate.*' in their first sentence.

Well, in the past I sometimes used to procrastinate a little. There were times when I used to put things off until the last minute, when completing an essay for university for example. But I realised that perhaps this wasn't the most effective way of working and so I started setting a strict schedule for all my projects well in advance and set myself personal deadlines. Using a schedule has really helped me and I'm much better organised now and able to take on more projects at the same time.

b Underline any words or phrases in the extract in Exercise 4a that soften negatives and emphasise positives.

c ▶5.9 Complete the second candidate's response using *always*, *really* or *very*. Listen again and check your answers.

Hmm. My weaknesses? Let me think. Well, in answer to your question you mentioned that the staff here use Apple Macintosh computers. I am not (1) _____ familiar with Apple Macs and I'm used to using Windows. However, I managed to learn how to use a number of programs (2) _____ quickly on my own and I'm sure I'd get used to using Apple Macs (3) _____ quickly. I (4) _____ enjoy using computers and new gadgets, and I'm (5) _____ keen to learn how to use new technology.

d ▶5.9 Complete the third candidate's response by adding the words in the box. Listen again and check your answers.

| ~~a bit of~~ a little   a lot of   as ... as possible |
| extremely   occasionally   very |

                             a bit of

Weaknesses? Well, I can be ʌa workaholic and always get involved in every project that I work on. I'm happy to spend time and energy making sure that every project is successful. So, when I feel that other members of the team might not be working as hard, I can get frustrated. I'm aware of this problem, and I try to solve situations like this by being positive and enthusiastic.

e In pairs, discuss the following questions.

1 What structure did the first candidate use to describe a problem that no longer exists? Why is this structure especially suitable here?
2 What tense did she use to show the present result of her new strategy for dealing with this problem?
3 The second candidate said that he wasn't familiar with Apple Macs. What structure did he use to show what he *is* familiar with? What structure did he use to show how he would become familiar with Apple Macs in the future?
4 What modal verb did the third candidate use to show that her weaknesses don't always affect her?

f Rewrite these descriptions of weaknesses using the expressions in brackets to soften the negative information.

1 I have difficulty making decisions. (occasionally / a little)
    _____

2 I used to be too stubborn and it was hard to get me to change my mind. (a bit / sometimes)
    _____

3 When working on projects I am a 'big picture' person. This means that I miss some details. (from time to time / might / minor)
    _____

g ▶5.10 Match the sentences (1–3) in Exercise 4f to the rest of the candidates' answers (a–c). Listen and check your answers.

a   *A former colleague of mine told me that I was becoming difficult to work with. Well, ever since then I have put significant effort into my teamworking skills and now I actively ask for advice and suggestions from my colleagues when making decisions. Last year I was even asked to chair weekly staff meetings while our boss was away on business.*

b   *This is because I pay a lot of attention to detail and make sure that every single decision I make is the best decision possible. Basically, I'm somebody who carefully considers all of the available options before making a choice.*

c   *I've been aware of this for some time. So now when I'm managing a project I make sure that I have the support I need to keep an eye on specific minor details, leaving me free to concentrate on managing the entire project. I think successful management is about getting the right team together and then completely trusting them to do the job you've given them.*

1 _____   2 _____   3 _____

h   Underline words in the extracts in Exercise 4g that emphasise positives.

i   ▶5.11 Listen to a candidate, Adam, answering the question, '*What is it about your job that you dislike?*' In pairs, discuss the techniques he uses to turn his response into an impressive positive answer.

j   Match the negative expressions (1–6) to the more positive expressions (a–f). Which expressions did Adam use in Exercise 4i?

1 I'm bored with my job. It's too easy.	a I enjoy a great deal about my current job.
2 I can't stand dealing with customers.	b I'm keen to develop my practical skills.
3 The place where I work is too small.	c I'm looking for an opportunity to contribute these skills to a larger organisation such as yours.
4 I don't have many professional skills.	d I feel I'm best suited to working behind the scenes.
5 I only know the theory.	e I'm seeking fresh challenges.
6 There are things that I don't like at work.	f I'm seeking the possibility to develop further professionally.

k   In pairs, take turns to ask and answer the following questions. Use the techniques and expressions in this section to soften any negatives and emphasise the positives in your responses.

1   What are your weaknesses?
2   Tell me about something you have found difficult at university/work.
3   What skills do you need to improve?
4   What kinds of decisions are most difficult for you to make?
5   What did you dislike about university / your last job?

Asking questions of your own

It is very common for interviewers to close an interview by asking if the candidate has any questions they would like to ask. People who ask good questions demonstrate real interest in and knowledge of the job.

5 a In pairs, discuss the following questions.

1 What sort of information should you try to find out during your interview?
2 What questions would you ask in an interview in your country?
3 Are there any questions you wouldn't ask? Why not?
4 Would you ask about salary?

b Read the following extract from an article about asking questions in an interview. Which do you think is the best question?

Questions to ask

Job hunters are always being told to ask one or two killer questions in an interview. But how exactly do you go about doing this?

It's important to consider the culture of the organisation you are hoping to join and the personality of the interviewer. Be careful to adopt the right tone and convey a positive attitude. You want to ensure this opportunity works for you, not against you.

Pick and choose from the following list of tried-and-tested questions.

a *What are the most / least enjoyable aspects of the role?*
b *You mentioned there would be a lot of researching. Could you tell me what your most successful employees find most satisfying about this part of the role?*
c *What are the most important issues that you think the organisation faces?*
d *Could you tell me more about the training opportunities you offer?*
e *Could you tell me how performance is measured and reviewed?*
f *Would there be a chance for promotion in the future?*
g *Do you have any doubts about whether I am suited to this position?*

C Match the questions in the article (a–g) to the following expert advice (1–7).

1 This question can highlight that you are keen to develop your skills and add further value to a company. _d_
2 This question can emphasise your determination to make progress and to do so over the long term. ____
3 This question can demonstrate your listening skills, and associates you with being successful in the role, as well as finding it satisfying. ____
4 This question can show that you like to know what sort of challenge you are going to face and that you like to get properly prepared for it. ____
5 This question can demonstrate that you appreciate the importance of delivering results. ____
6 This question can show that you are interested in the employer as well as the job. It will be clear you have done some research, done some thinking, and are now keen to hear their analysis. ____
7 This question is a rather bold way of emphasising some of your strengths. It suggests you are open to constructive criticism and willing to learn from the experience of others. In addition, it gives you a real chance to address any weaknesses the employer may think you have. Finally, it allows you to finish on a high, restating why you think you are the right person. ____

d Look at four versions of the same question (a–d). In pairs, discuss the following questions.

1 Which version is the most assertive?
2 Which version is the most delicate/tentative?
3 Which would you use?

I noticed from your brochure that you are actively involved in several projects to support the local community.

a *If I were to work for you, would that be something I could get involved in?*
b *If I work for you, will that be something I can get involved in?*
c *If I worked for you, would that be something I could get involved in?*
d *If I work for you, is that something I can get involved in?*

e Complete the following candidate's questions with your own ideas.

1 Could you tell me more about _____ ?
2 What are the most important _____ ?
3 Could you tell me how _____ ?
4 Would there be a chance _____ ?
5 Do you have _____ ?

f It is important to show you are listening actively to the interviewer's response to your question. In pairs, take turns to ask and answer your questions in Exercise 5e. Remember to show you are listening actively by:

- keeping eye contact with the interviewer;
- nodding your head;
- making noises and short comments to show you understand (*OK* / *Really?* / *I see*);
- paraphrasing what the interviewer has just told you (*so you're saying* …).

Dealing with telephone interviews

Employers often use telephone interviews for recruitment, as a way of screening large numbers of applicants before selecting a smaller pool of candidates for face-to-face interviews.

6 a In pairs, discuss the following questions.

1 Would you prefer to have an interview face-to-face or on the telephone?
2 Why is it increasingly popular for initial interviews to be held over the phone?
3 What are the advantages of telephone interviews for the candidate?
4 When is the best time to arrange a telephone interview?
5 Why should you smile during a telephone interview?
6 What is the candidate's main aim in most telephone interviews?

b Read the following article and compare the advice with your answers in Exercise 6a.

Tackling telephone interviews

It is common practice these days for initial first interviews to be held over the phone. The main reason for this is that it significantly reduces the cost for employers, who often use telephone interviews as a method of filtering candidates before moving on to face-to-face interviews. Telephone interviews also have benefits for the applicants as well. As well as the obvious financial saving, an applicant may feel more relaxed within their own environment surrounded by their CV and research materials to aid them. You also don't have to wear a suit!

It is essential that you organise a time for a telephone interview that is convenient for you. You should suggest a time when you are unlikely to be disturbed, when you are in a quiet environment and you are confident that you have prepared sufficiently to convince the interviewer you are the right person for the job, or at least a second interview.

During the interview you should:

- smile, as this will help you to relax and project a positive image to the interviewer and will alter the tone of your voice.
- speak slowly and clearly. It's perfectly acceptable to take your time when answering questions.
- give short, memorable answers.
- use the person's title (Mr or Ms and their last name). Only use a first name if you are invited to.
- keep a copy of your CV open next to you, so that it's at your fingertips when you need it.
- have a pen and paper next to you so that you can make notes if you need to.

Remember that your goal is to try and set up a face-to-face interview. At the end of the interview ask if it would be possible to meet in person.

c Alex Mencken has recently applied for a number of administrative assistant jobs with theatres. A potential employer calls him for a telephone interview. However, as Alex has applied to many theatres he cannot remember the specific details about the theatre when he receives the unexpected call. In pairs, discuss what you would do in Alex's situation.

d ▶5.12 Listen to the telephone conversation between Alex and John Bradshaw from King's Theatre. What do you think of the way Alex dealt with the conversation? Do you think he handled the conversation well?

e ▶5.12 Listen again and complete the conversation.

John: *Hello. Can I speak to Alex Mencken please?*
Alex: *This is Alex. (1) _____ ?*
John: *Hello, Alex. My name is John Bradshaw and I'm calling from King's Theatre regarding your recent application for a position with us. Is this a good time for you?*
Alex: *Oh, (2) _____ . Unfortunately I have about ten minutes before I have to leave. Is that enough time, or can you call back later this afternoon?*
John: *That would be fine. (3) _____ ? I'm free after 2pm.*
Alex: *How about 2.30?*
John: *Perfect. I'll call you at 2.30.*
Alex: *Great. (4) _____ .*
John: *Yes. So do I. Speak to you later. Goodbye.*
Alex: *Bye.*

f ▶5.13 At 2.30pm Alex is sitting comfortably, he has thoroughly researched the position at King's Theatre and he has a copy of his CV in front of him. When John Bradshaw calls for the interview, Alex is feeling well-prepared. Listen to an extract from the interview and answer the following questions.

1 What responsibilities does John mention?
2 Would the successful applicant receive help to do this job?
3 Why does Alex have problems hearing John?
4 How does King's Theatre support new talent?

g ▶5.13 Listen again and tick (✔) the phrases you hear.

1 *I'm sorry, could you say that again?* ✔
2 *I didn't quite catch what you said.*
3 *I'm having trouble hearing you. Can you hear me clearly?*
4 *Could you explain what you mean by ...?*
5 *So, if I understand you correctly ...*
6 *Do you mean ...?*
7 *Could you elaborate a little on ...?*
8 *Could you tell me what that would involve?*

h Decide whether the phrases (1–8) in Exercise 6g ask for repetition (R), clarification (C) or more information (I).

1 _R_   2 __   3 __   4 __   5 __   6 __   7 __   8 __

i ▶5.14 Complete the following extracts from telephone interviews using the phrases in Exercise 6g. Listen and check your answers.

1 **Candidate:** <u>Could you explain what you mean by</u> *piece rates?*
   Interviewer: *Piecework is a form of performance-related pay, where you would be paid a fixed piece rate for each unit you produce.*
2 **Candidate:** *I'm sorry, could you say that again, as* _____ *?*
   Interviewer: *Yes of course. My name is Mr Johnson and I'm calling to discuss your application for an internship here at Ariel Publishers.*
3 **Candidate:** _____ *that when the company is busy I would be required to work overtime?*
   Interviewer: *Yes. But of course overtime rates are higher than normal pay.*
4 **Candidate:** _____
   Interviewer: *Yes, I can hear you perfectly this end, although if you can't hear me well, perhaps I'll try and call you back on a landline.*
5 **Candidate:** *Your advertisement mentions administrative work.* _____
   Interviewer: *Well, basically it means keeping our records up-to-date and sending a weekly email to our clients.*
6 **Candidate:** _____ *, what you're saying is the job may involve some overtime?*
   Interviewer: *Yes, but you would be paid extra for this.*

j In pairs, practise the dialogues in Exercise 6i.

k In pairs, role play a telephone interview. Sit back-to-back.

Student A, you are the interviewer. Interview the candidate for a job you know well. Use the following phrases.

> Let me start by outlining the main aspects of the position and then we'll see how closely your skills and experience match the job. OK?
>
> One of the main responsibilities of the post holder is to ...
>
> Another part of the job is ...
>
> The role would also require ...
>
> What experience do you have in the area of ...?
>
> Tell me about a time when you had to ...
>
> How do your skills and experience match the requirements for this position?

Student B, you are the candidate. Answer the questions honestly. Use the following clarification phrases.

> I'm sorry, could you say that again?
>
> I didn't quite catch what you said.
>
> Could you explain what you mean by ...?
>
> So, if I understand you correctly ...?
>
> Could you elaborate a little on ...?
>
> Could you tell me what that would involve?

After the interview, give feedback to each other. Swap roles and practise again.

l In pairs, tell your partner about a job you would like to be interviewed for. Look through units 4 and 5 and choose five questions to ask your partner, based on the job they have chosen. Then take turns to ask and answer your questions. Try to use the techniques from these units to make your answers as impressive as possible.

UNIT 6 Follow up

- Keeping in touch
- Handling rejection
- Dealing with job offers
- Negotiating terms and conditions

Keeping in touch

As soon as you've put the phone down or walked out of the interview room you can relax for a few moments. The interview is over. However, even though the interview is over, there is still a lot you can do to leave a positive impression on your prospective employer. It's important to start the follow-up process as soon as possible. Walking away and leaving the final stages of a job application to chance is a common mistake, but until you have been offered the job, the hunt is not over.

1 **a** **In pairs, discuss the following questions.**

1 What can you do after an interview to increase your chances of being offered the job?
2 How long should you wait to hear from the interviewer? What should you do if you don't hear from the interviewer after the interview?
3 What should you do if you're offered another job?

b **After the interview you should write down everything important that occurred in the interview while you can still remember what happened. Why could it be useful to review your performance in this way?**

c **In pairs, think of an interview you have had in the past and discuss the following questions.**

1 What questions were you asked?
2 Were you expecting them?
3 Did you feel you projected yourself well in terms of body language?
4 Did you manage to put across your key skills and achievements successfully?
5 Did you give any negative information about yourself?
6 Do you need more practice in closing the interview positively?
7 Generally, what could you improve about your interview technique?
8 Did you ask yourself these questions after the interview?

d ▶6.1 After her interview at Futerra, Silvia Carnali meets up with her friend Sophie to talk about how it went. Listen to the beginning of the conversation and answer the following questions.

1 Did Silvia's interview go well?
2 What does Sophie suggest Silvia does next?
3 What is Silvia worried about?

e In pairs, discuss the following advice on writing a follow-up letter. For each suggestion, think of reasons why it is a good idea.

1 Send the letter within 24 hours of the interview.
2 Refer to specific things that the interviewer mentioned during the interview.
3 Demonstrate that you are excited about the job, can do it, and want it.
4 Explain how you would be able to contribute to the success of the company.
5 Include any important information you forgot to mention during the interview.

f ▶6.2 Listen to the rest of Silvia and Sophie's conversation and compare your answers in Exercise 1e with Sophie's ideas.

g Complete Silvia's follow-up letter by putting the following sentences in the correct order.

a ... the challenges of the post. Having discussed the role of Junior Consultant with you in greater depth, I am confident in my ability to meet these challenges and believe I can make a significant ...

b With this in mind I have already developed some practical ideas for making the Futerra newsletter and website more user-friendly, which would lead to closer communication with key clients. Please feel free to contact me if you require any further information ...

c As mentioned when we met, I am keen to use the research conducted as part of my Master's degree on sustainability to enhance Futerra's identity, while at the same time meeting ...

d ... as I feel my qualifications and experience make me ideally suited to work in this area. I recognise the importance of maintaining relationships and ensuring that newsletters and invitations are sent out on a timely basis.

e ... regarding my qualifications, experience or suitability for the position. I look forward ...

f ... contribution to the close team at Futerra. I am particularly interested in the projects you mentioned during the interview which involve working with influential business leaders, ...

g ... at Futerra. I appreciate the time you and your team took in telling me about the specific aspects of the job and the valuable work Futerra is doing.

h Dear Mr Lewis, Thank you very much for taking the time to interview me today for the Junior Consultant position ...

i ... to hearing from you soon, and thank you again for meeting me. Yours sincerely, Silvia Carnali

1	_h_	3	___	5	___	7	___	9	___
2	___	4	___	6	___	8	___		

h The letter in Exercise 1g is one long paragraph. Show where new paragraphs could begin by writing // in the text. Use the following structure to help you.

Greeting

Paragraph 1: Reason for writing (thanking the interviewer for the interview and showing that you appreciated the opportunity and were impressed by the company)

Paragraph 2: The job (restating your interest in the position, showing you understand the demands and challenges of the position and stating how and why you feel you are confident you can meet these)

Paragraph 3: Reflection and extra information (demonstrating that you have thought about what was said during the interview and have already started thinking of ways of approaching the job)

Paragraph 4: Final comments (expressing enthusiasm towards the job and inviting the possibility of a second interview)

Formal ending

Signature

i Complete the following table using the phrases in the box. You will need to use one phrase twice.

> As mentioned when we met ...
> Having discussed the role with you in greater depth ...
> I am confident in my ability to meet the challenges ...
> I am particularly interested in the projects that you talked about during the interview
> I appreciate the time you and the team took in telling me about the specific aspects of the job
> I believe I can make a significant contribution towards ...
> I feel I am perfectly suited for ...
> I look forward to hearing from you
> Thank you for taking the time to discuss ...
> This helped me gain a better understanding of ...

1 Demonstrates appreciation of the interview	2 Demonstrates interest and enthusiasm towards the position
3 Demonstrates confidence in your ability to do the job	4 Demonstrates that you paid attention to what was said
	As mentioned when we met ...

j Complete the following extracts from follow-up letters using the phrases in Exercise 1i.

1 _____ the insurance broker position with me. After meeting with you and discussing the company's operations, I am further convinced that my background and skills coincide well with your needs.

2 I would like to thank you for talking with me about the Research Assistant position at Mendoza. _____ , and learning more about me.

3 The information you provided about the planned new product line was particularly interesting. _____ the company's goals and objectives.

4 With my recent experience in climbing and mountaineering _____ the position of Expedition Leader. After the interview, I am even more excited at the prospect of using my skills at Global Adventures.

5 You mentioned that a hiring decision would be made within two weeks. _____ . If you require any additional information from me in the meantime, please do not hesitate to contact me.

Handling rejection

Learning from failure

Almost nobody has succeeded in getting every job they have ever applied for. There will almost certainly be times when, despite your best efforts, you don't get the job.

2 a ▶6.3 Job seeker Paul has just received a rejection letter from a bank he was hoping to work for. Listen to Paul talking to his friend Carmen and mark the following statements True (T) or False (F).

1 Paul was rejected because he didn't really want the job.
   _F_

2 Carmen thinks Paul was rejected because he wasn't a strong candidate. ___

3 Carmen thinks interviewers sometimes already know who is likely to get a job before the interview happens. ___

4 Carmen thinks a candidate who already knows the interviewers has a good chance of getting the job. ___

5 Carmen thinks that most interviews are open and fair. ___

6 Paul has written to request feedback. ___

7 Carmen thinks Paul still has a chance of working for the bank. ___

b In pairs, discuss the following questions.

1 Have you ever been rejected for a job? How did it feel?

2 Think of as many reasons as you can why a candidate may not be offered a job after an interview.

3 Some people handle failure by forgetting all about their unsuccessful application and turning immediately to the next one. Others spend a lot of time analysing what went wrong and what they could have done better. What are the advantages and disadvantages of each approach? Which approach do you use?

4 Have you ever requested feedback after an unsuccessful interview? Was it a useful experience?

Requesting feedback

In order for your next job application to be more successful it is essential to know why you didn't get this job. Did somebody else manage to convince the employer that they were the best person for the job? What skills or experience did the other applicant have that you lacked? Or was it you that made a mistake during your interview? Reviewing your performance will help you to answer some of these questions, but it is also perfectly acceptable to ask an employer why you didn't get the job.

3 a **Complete Paul's letter requesting feedback about his interview using the phrases in the box.**

> I am confident
> I am grateful
> ~~I greatly appreciated the opportunity~~
> I would very much appreciate
> Obviously I am disappointed
> Thank you very much in advance

Dear Mr Brooker,

Thank you for your letter informing me that my recent application for employment with your bank has been unsuccessful.

(1) _I greatly appreciated the opportunity_ to meet with you and your team.

(2) _____ for the time you took to talk to me about the position. (3) _____ to have been unsuccessful this time, as I felt my skills and experience matched the requirements for the job.

(4) _____ it if you could explain in greater detail why my application was unsuccessful on this occasion.

(5) _____ this information will help me to identify areas which I need to work on in order to successfully gain employment in future.

(6) _____ for your time on this matter.

Yours sincerely,

Paul Kristiansen

b **Read the letter Paul received from the bank in response. Why was he rejected?**

Dear Paul

Many thanks for your letter requesting feedback. As I'm sure you'll understand, we had a very strong field of candidates. Although we considered your application to be very strong, our recruitment procedure enabled us to assess each candidate as objectively as possible, and we chose the candidate who scored most highly in our assessment.

There were many things that impressed us about your application. Your qualifications are excellent, and you have some good experience in this sector. You gave good answers to many questions, particularly our question at the beginning about customer service, for which you gave several excellent examples.

The main reason why your application was less successful was that your work experience is fairly limited, and we felt that you would benefit from some months in a more junior position before you are ready for a job involving managing people and budgets. When we asked you about your leadership skills, you gave a general answer rather than the specific example that we needed. We suspect that you do in fact have such skills, but because you did not illustrate these at the interview, we felt unable to know for certain. This leads us to a more general point: your answers were often short and lacking examples. We would recommend you plan your examples more carefully before your next interview.

You did create a positive impression on us, and have good potential to be a strong and useful member of a team such as ours. If you are interested in applying for a more junior position, I encourage you to consider responding to the job advertisement attached. I realise this might not be your ideal job, but as I mentioned above, we felt you would be a much stronger candidate for a management position after you had such experience.

Thank you again for your application, and we wish you well in your career.

Charlie Brooker

c In pairs, discuss the following questions.

1 What did Paul do well in his interview? What did he do badly?
2 What advice is Paul given? Do you think this is good advice?
3 Why do you think the interviewers didn't use his good examples of customer service skills to guess about his leadership skills?
4 Do you think Mr Brooker genuinely wants Paul to apply for the junior job, or do all unsuccessful candidates get the same advice?
5 What would you do if you were Paul? Would you apply for the more junior position or would you wait for another management position to be available?

d Write a letter requesting feedback for a real job for which you were rejected, or for an invented one. Use expressions from the letter in Exercise 3a.

Dealing with job offers

Accepting the job

Congratulations! You have been offered a job. Even if you have accepted a job over the phone, or in person, it is important to write an acceptance letter to confirm the details of employment and to formally accept the job offer.

4 a In pairs, discuss the following questions.

1 What should you consider before accepting a job offer?
2 Why is it good practice to write a formal letter accepting or declining a position you are offered?

b ▶6.4 A few days after his telephone interview, Alex Mencken receives a telephone call from King's Theatre offering him the position. Listen to the conversation. How do you think Alex handled the conversation? Why didn't he accept straight away?

c ▶6.4 Complete the conversation using the words in the box. Listen again and check your answers.

consider	contact	decision	latest	meantime	offer
position	salary	~~speaking~~	time		

Alex: *Hello. Alex* (1) ___speaking___ .

John: *Hello, Alex. It's John Bradshaw from King's Theatre. I'm delighted to tell you that after careful consideration we would like to offer you the (2) _____ of administrative assistant.*

Alex: *Thank you very much. That's very good news.*

John: *As we discussed during the interview, we are happy to offer you a starting (3) _____ of £20,000.*

Alex: *That's great. I'd like to take some (4) _____ to (5) _____ your (6) _____ . Is it okay if I (7) _____ you with a (8) _____ by tomorrow at the (9) _____ ?*

John: *Yes. That's absolutely fine. And if you have any questions in the (10) _____ , please feel free to give me a call.*

d In pairs, practise the conversation in Exercise 4c. Swap roles and practise again.

e ▶6.5 Listen to Alex discussing the job offer with his friend Ella and answer the following questions.

1 Is Alex worried about relocating to London?
2 Does he feel he would be able to get on with the boss and the rest of the team?
3 Is he happy with the salary that he has been offered?
4 What issues does he still need to clarify before accepting the position?
5 What does Ella think Alex should do after accepting the position by phone?

f ▶6.6 Ella goes on to give Alex a lot of advice on how to write an acceptance letter and what to include. Put Ella's advice (a–e) into the most logical order. Listen and check your answers. What do you think of the advice?

a Express how much you are looking forward to starting the job. ___
b Thank whoever made you the job offer, and then make it clear that you have decided to accept it. _1_
c Repeat any instructions you were given during the interview such as your starting date, working hours, etc. ___
d Request clarification in your acceptance letter of any terms of employment that were vague or that concerned you. ___
e Restate the terms of employment as you understood them, including hours per week, salary and benefits. ___

g Alex called John Bradshaw at King's Theatre to clarify terms and conditions of service. Afterwards, he wrote a formal letter of acceptance. Separate Alex's acceptance letter into five paragraphs using the plan in Exercise 4f. Mark the beginning of each new paragraph with //.

> Dear Mr Bradshaw, Thank you for your offer of employment as Administrative Assistant at King's Theatre. As we discussed on the phone yesterday, I am delighted to accept your offer and look forward to beginning work at King's Theatre. I am pleased to accept your offer at a salary of £20,000 annually. As we agreed, my starting date will be July 29 to enable me to complete the training programme that I have enrolled for. I also understand that I will receive full company pay and benefits during the 8-week long training programme as the skills I will acquire on the course will be applicable and useful within my new role at King's Theatre. During the interview we did not discuss holiday entitlement and I hope you will be able to clarify exactly how much holiday leave I will be entitled to. Thank you again for offering me this wonderful opportunity, and do let me know if there is any additional information or paperwork you need prior to this. I very much look forward to joining you and the theatre team on July 29. Yours sincerely, Alex Mencken

h Underline three phrases in the letter referring to previous discussions. What other phrases in the letter could you use in your own letter of acceptance? For example, *Thank you for your offer of employment as* …

i What is the effect of the words in bold in the following extract from Alex's letter?

Thank you again for offering me this **wonderful** opportunity, and **do** let me know if there is any additional information or paperwork you need prior to this. I **very much** look forward to joining you **and the theatre team** on July 29.

j Write a letter of acceptance for a job you would like. Try to make your letter positive and enthusiastic.

Withdrawing from consideration

When you accept a job offer you will need to notify other prospective employers that you are withdrawing your name from their consideration. As soon as you have made a decision you should politely inform all other employers that you have applied for work with. Make every effort to speak to your contact in person rather than leaving a voicemail message. After you have spoken to your contact, follow up with a written confirmation.

5 a ▶6.7 **After Alex has accepted the job at King's Theatre, he telephones the Cromwell Theatre to politely withdraw from their application process. Complete the conversation using the phrases in the box. Listen and check your answers.**

Could you put me through	I was very impressed by your team
I'm calling as I've been offered	It's the least I could do
I just wanted to let you know	That's very kind of you

Alex: *Hello. This is Alex Mencken. (1) Could you put me through to Karl Osborne please?*

Receptionist: *Yes, of course. I'll just put you on hold for a minute, and put you through.*

Karl: *Hello, Alex. What can I do for you? I'm afraid we haven't made a decision yet as we're still in the process of interviewing candidates for the position.*

Alex: *Yes, I know. Actually, (2) _____ a job elsewhere, which I have accepted.*

Karl: *I see.*

Alex: *(3) _____ . I also wanted to say that I really enjoyed meeting you. (4) _____ and the working environment at the Cromwell.*

Karl: *Thank you for saying so. I would say that we were also impressed by your interview and I'm sorry to hear that you've accepted another job. But I understand your decision. I wish you the very best of luck.*

Alex: *Thank you very much.*

Karl: *And if things don't work out, make sure that you give me a ring and I'll see if we've got anything we can offer you.*

Alex: *(5) _____ . I will do.*

Karl: *Thanks for letting us know like this.*

Alex: *(6) _____ . Thank you for giving me the chance to talk about possible work at the theatre.*

b **In pairs, role play telephoning to withdraw from consideration. Before you start, decide what job you have applied for.**

Student A, you are the candidate. Call the employer to withdraw from consideration from the recruitment process. Use the expressions in Exercise 5a.

Student B, you are the employer. You interviewed Student A for a job, and are disappointed that they are withdrawing. Be polite and try to encourage them to consider working for you in the future.

Swap roles and practise again.

c Match the spoken expressions (1–6) to the equivalent formal written expressions (a–f).

1	I have accepted another job	a	I recently submitted an application for the vacant Administrative Assistant position
2	It's a job that will let me use my skills and is what I want to do	b	The position closely matches my abilities and personal career aims
3	I applied for the Administrative Assistant job	c	I am writing to withdraw from consideration for the position
4	I no longer want to be considered for the job	d	I have decided to accept a position elsewhere
5	I really enjoyed meeting you and the rest of the office	e	I wish you and your team the best of success
6	Good luck in the future	f	I greatly enjoyed meeting you and your team

d Complete Alex's letter of withdrawal using all or part of the formal expressions in Exercise 5c.

Dear Mr Osborne,

I am writing to thank you for including me in the interview process as you seek candidates for your (1) *vacant Administrative Assistant position* . (2) _____ you and members of your staff and was impressed by your operation at the Cromwell Theatre.

However, as I explained when we spoke this morning, (3) _____ .
(4) _____ which I believe (5) _____ .

I wish you and the staff at the Cromwell Theatre the (6) _____ .

Yours sincerely,

Alex Mencken

e Now write a letter of withdrawal based on the role play in Exercise 5b, using formal the expressions in Exercise 5c.

Declining an offer

The decision to decline a job offer is usually made because you have received another offer that matches your interests and career goals better.

6 a In pairs, discuss the following questions.

1 Why is it important to decline a job offer that you do not want politely?
2 How much information do you need to give when declining a job offer?
3 When should you decline a job offer?

b ▶6.8 Tomasz Filipek, a young graduate from Poland, recently moved to London and applied for a number of different jobs when he arrived. Tomasz was fortunate and received a number of job offers, including one that he decided to accept. Now he is calling the other companies to politely decline their offers of employment. Listen to one of these conversations and complete the following notes.

1 Company: _____
2 Contact name: _____
3 Position applied for: _____
4 Positive things about the company: _____
5 Reason for declining the position: _____

c ▶ **6.8** Listen again and complete Tomasz's letter declining the job offer using words from the conversation.

> Dear Ms Johnson,
>
> Thank you for extending the offer for the position of Graphic Designer. I very much (1) _appreciate_ the time and effort you and your team (2) _____ explaining the position and your agency's specific goals. I was very (3) _____ by the advertising campaigns you are working on for major retailers.
>
> (4) _____ , after much thought and careful deliberation, I have decided not to (5) _____ your offer. Although this would have certainly been an excellent (6) _____ for me, I have decided to accept another position, which more closely matches my specific skills and career goals.
>
> I wish you and Future Designs continued success for the future.
>
> Thank you again for your time and consideration.
>
> Yours sincerely,
>
> Tomasz Filipek

d In pairs, role play telephoning to decline an offer. Before you start, decide what job you have applied for.

Student A, you are the candidate.

Student B, you are the employer.

Swap roles and practise again.

e Underline useful phrases from the letter in Exercise 6c, which you could use in your own letter. For example, _Thank you for extending the offer for the position of_ ...

f Write a formal letter declining an offer using the phrases in Exercise 6e, based on your role play in Exercise 6d.

Negotiating terms and conditions

When negotiating a salary deal, you are trying to persuade your future employer to give you the best deal possible, so you must be as polite and diplomatic as possible. You should use tentative language and formal English.

7 a In pairs, discuss the following questions.

1 Is it common in your country to negotiate salary and conditions of employment?
2 What advice would you give someone entering into salary negotiations?

b ▶ **6.9** Listen to two job seekers, Andy and Nick, negotiating a pay deal with their future employers. Who negotiates a better deal?

c ▶ **6.10** Listen to two recruitment experts, Grace and Oliver, discussing Andy and Nick's negotiation strategies. What advice do they give? Do you agree with them?

d ►6.9 Complete the conversation using one word in each gap. Listen again and check your answers.

Employer: *What sort of salary are you looking for, Nick?*

Nick 1: *Well, I know you are a well-established company with a reputation for looking after your people well, so I (1) _____ you will be offering employment at the market rate.*

Employer: *Yes, that's very true, but we have to start somewhere, so tell me, what are you expecting?*

Nick 2: *Perhaps you could tell me what the range is for this position, as I (2) _____ be tempted to overprice myself if I give a figure.*

Employer: *Well, the range for this post is between $42,000 and $44,000.*

Nick 3: *I see. Given that I have five years' full-time experience in this field, and have an MA, how far up the range (3) _____ you be able to offer someone like myself?*

Employer: *We were thinking in the region of $43,000.*

Nick 4: *… mmm …*

Employer: *But in your case, considering your specific previous employment experience we could offer $43,000 plus a $2,000 starting bonus.*

Nick 5: *Thank you. (4) _____ you tell me how often pay is reviewed here?*

Employer: *Normally once a year. The next pay review is due in October.*

Nick 6: *(5) _____ I be entitled to a pay review at this point – subject, of course, to my satisfactory performance in the position?*

Employer: *Yes, that's reasonable.*

e Match Nick's responses (1−6) in Exercise 7d to the negotiation techniques (a−f).

a Remind the employer of your key skills and relevant experience. _3_
b Establish the employer's range for the position. ___
c Avoid being the first person to state a salary figure. ___
d Before you accept an offer establish if and when your salary will be reviewed in future. ___
e Don't automatically accept the first offer that is made. ___
f Before you accept an offer clarify your queries about the terms and conditions. ___

f Nick uses formal language to negotiate a better salary. Complete the formal versions of the sentences in bold by rearranging the words in brackets.

1 **How much can you pay me?**
Could you tell me what (position / the / is / range / this / for) _____
_____ ?
How much would you be able to offer someone (my / experience / of / level / with) _____ ?

2 **As I've got a lot of experience, will you pay me more?**
Taking my experience into account, (higher / consider / a / would / amount / you) _____ ?

3 **I think I can get more money doing the same job elsewhere.**
I've done some research into equivalent jobs within the sector, and feel that your (below / current / market / position / this / for / is / offer / the / rate) _____
_____ .

g In pairs, practise your negotiation skills in a game.

Student A, you are the employer. Try and get the candidate to agree to the lowest starting salary with minimal additional benefits. Use the role cards on page 96.

Student B, you are the candidate. Use language and techniques from this section to achieve the best possible terms and conditions of service. Use the role cards on page 104.

Before you start, decide on the company and the job. Swap roles and play the game again.

Rules

- The employer earns points by managing to keep the starting salary as low as possible and by not agreeing to too many additional benefits (although remember that you do want to employ this applicant).
- The applicant earns points by achieving as high a starting salary as possible and by gaining additional benefits.
- The employer and applicant do not know how many points the other person can earn from each negotiation issue. The person with the most points at the end of the negotiation is the winner.

AUDIOSCRIPT

◼ 1.1

Sophie: Hey Silvia. How are you? What have you been up to? I haven't seen you for ages.

Silvia: I'm fine, Sophie. I'm actually looking for a job at the moment.

Sophie: Yeah? So how's it going?

Silvia: Not that great, to be honest. I've got a few ideas for possible jobs but I'm not really sure what sort of work I want to do, or what I'd be really good at.

Sophie: I see. In my experience you've got to work out what you want to do before you start thinking about where you want to work. So, start by thinking about the things you like doing, or what you're interested in.

Silvia: Well, I'm interested in sustainability and I enjoy working with people.

Sophie: Exactly. So you'd probably enjoy a job that included both of these things. Then, after you've worked out your interests, the next step is to think about the skills you've got that can be used in almost any job, things like communication and people skills. Everything that you've managed to do successfully at work or university needed skills to get these things done. These are your transferable skills.

Silvia: But how do I work out what my transferable skills are?

Sophie: I try to think about something I've done that was successful, where my actions have made a difference, and then try to identify the skills I used.

Silvia: Hmm. I can do that, I think.

Sophie: Also, a lot of people these days use personality tests to find out more about the type of person they are and the types of jobs that are suited to them. There are quite a lot of them on the Internet if you're interested.

Silvia: That sounds interesting. I'll give it a go, and see what it comes up with.

Sophie: Okay, but don't take these tests too seriously – they're just there to give you some ideas and suggestions. At the end of the day, the only person who really knows who you are and what type of job is right for you is you. And remember, it's not just about finding a job that you'd be good at. You need to find a job that you'll enjoy, one that you'll love doing.

◼ 1.2

Jack: So, Federico. What's all this about you moving jobs?

Federico: Well, yes, I've just decided to start looking for a new job. I love my current job, and my colleagues are great, but if I'm going to get more experience, I'll have to go somewhere else.

Jack: Sure you can't get that experience where you are?

Federico: No. Our company's too small. I need to go somewhere bigger.

Jack: Any idea where?

Federico: Well, I've got a few companies in mind.

Jack: And have you got the skills and experience these companies are looking for?

Federico: Well, I've got the qualifications they're looking for. When it comes to skills and experience, I think I can demonstrate that I'm very adaptable. I don't mind working late or at weekends, and I'll have a go at anything, I pick things up very quickly.

Jack: That's true.

Federico: I'm also good at coming up with new ideas and suggesting alternative solutions. That sort of thing.

Jack: Yeah, I remember when we used to work together, you used to stick notes with new ideas everywhere. Your desk was such a mess and you never knew where anything was. The desk of a creative genius, I guess!

Federico: Well, the desk is still a mess, but at least I know where everything is now!

Jack: Well, it sounds like you've got a lot to offer.

Federico: Yes, although the main company I'm interested in is looking for someone who can speak a bit of Mandarin, and I've never even been to China. I'd love to be able to speak Mandarin, though.

Jack: So what are you going to do about it?

Federico: Well, actually I've already started taking lessons, and I've started listening to Chinese language podcasts while I travel on the bus. I'm hoping that my commitment might help convince the company to take me on.

Jack: That's impressive. How's it going?

Federico: It's tough, but if I want to get a new job, I've got to make the effort.

◼ 1.3

Sophie: So, how's the job-hunting going?

Silvia: Well, I haven't got very far, to be honest. I'm struggling to work out what my transferable skills are.

Sophie: Well, you've done so much, Silvia. I'm sure you've got lots of skills that would be useful in almost any job. Why don't you tell me some things you've done and then we can work out what transferable skills you've got?

Silvia: Well, I applied for my MA course while I was working in Africa, and even managed to start doing some research for the course before I came back to England.

Sophie: So you're clearly quite good at planning. And what were you doing in Africa? I'm sure that you developed lots of skills while you were there that will help you get a job.

Silvia: I worked for an NGO as part of a large team with people from all over the world. We all lived together and shared a bathroom. The work was quite varied and I was given different tasks to complete each week.

Sophie: Like what?

Silvia: Well, for example, on the project our main aim was to educate local people about the need for reforestation. We tried putting up posters, but this didn't have much of an effect. We needed to find a better way to communicate this message. Later on I talked to respected members of the community, and convinced them to talk to other people in the village. This approach was far more effective.

Sophie: You've always been good at persuading other people!

Silvia: I guess you're right. When I was at university I was the communications officer of the student union and I was responsible for dealing with suppliers. I had to order food and drink for university concerts and so on. It was always possible to get a better deal if you were good on the phone. It wasn't just a question of being

persuasive though, it was really a case of being clear and expressing yourself well, making sure that everybody understood what I was saying.

Sophie: Okay. I think we've got lots to work on already. Now let's try and think about what you've said in terms of transferable skills …

◼ 1.4

1

This is easily the best way of finding a job. It's simply the biggest resource available. You can search through thousands of jobs and send your CV and cover letter to employers all over the world in minutes. You can even post your own CV online and help employers and headhunters find you. There are hundreds of networks, groups and special interest forums that you can sign up to, which can offer you advice and tell you about any job opportunities.

2

Nothing beats word of mouth and a personal recommendation. As the old saying goes, it's not what you know, it's who you know. If you want to get ahead and get the job you really want, then you've got to get to know someone who already works in the industry, someone who can recommend you for a job, or let you know of any openings. It might take time and effort, but if you want to be really successful, the best way to do it is by meeting the right people. Tell everyone you know you're looking for a job, tell them what area of work you're interested in and ask them to let you know if they can help you in any way.

3

Professional knowledge and advice can really improve your chances of getting a job. I've used this method throughout my entire career to help me find and secure the best jobs possible. Having an experienced consultant was especially useful when I moved abroad for work, as they really knew the legalities of the recruitment process in the country I was looking for work in. Of course, I had to pay for these services, but in some cases the employers themselves pay for the service. You've got to make sure you choose a well-established, reputable company as there are a lot of cowboys waiting to take your money.

4

Along with the Internet this is by far the most common way people hunt for job vacancies. Almost all publications have a weekly jobs section or supplement that provides a large selection of available jobs. It's also worth going back and looking at old editions as many jobs are often left unfilled.

5

Although this method takes courage, as you might often be faced with rejection, with the right approach this can also be a highly effective way of finding a job. It's also an excellent way of finding out more information about companies, job details and so on. Companies themselves are often very willing to let the public know all about what they do, who they employ and what work they carry out, but are rarely contacted directly as a resource. Calling a company to enquire about vacancies and offer your services can be a highly effective way of getting them interested in you enough to want to know more about you.

1.5

Patrick: Good morning. My name is Patrick Roberts. Can I speak to the head of Human Resources?

Receptionist: I'm afraid she's quite busy at the moment. Can I help you?

Patrick: I was just phoning to enquire whether there were any jobs going.

Receptionist: All our vacant positions are advertised on our website and in national newspapers. Vacancies do come up regularly, so I advise you to keep checking.

Patrick: Thank you very much for your time.

Receptionist: You're welcome and good luck.

Eryk: Good morning. I'm Eryk Pawlak. I would like to speak to Janet Robinson. Is she there?

Receptionist: She's quite busy at the moment. Can I help you?

Eryk: Thank you, but I'd rather talk to Ms Robinson, if that's okay.

Receptionist: Okay. Please hold and I'll try and put you through.

Eryk: Thank you.

Janet: Janet Robinson speaking. How can I help you?

Eryk: My name is Eryk Pawlak. I have considerable professional experience in the hotel industry. I have worked for a number of big hotels in Poland. The reason I'm calling, Ms Robinson, is that I have recently moved to London and I'm looking for an employment opportunity in a major hotel which will make use of my experience and language skills. Do you need employees who can speak a variety of languages?

Janet: Yes, we do.

Eryk: My mother tongue is Polish, but I can also speak Spanish, having worked for a big hotel in Spain. Are you looking for employees with international experience?

Janet: Yes. How much experience do you have?

Eryk: Recently I spent six months working for a hotel in Madrid. To begin with I mainly worked managing a team of cleaners and porters. However, my Spanish improved quickly and I was moved to reception, where I dealt with customers both face to face and on the phone. Are you looking for someone with experience such as this?

Janet: Do you have a degree?

Eryk: Yes, I have a degree in tourism. What background experience are you looking for?

Janet: We normally recruit people with a background in hotel management.

Eryk: Well, I have experience in this area and am keen to continue my professional development. I'm going to be close to your hotel this week. Would you be available to meet me to discuss my qualifications and experience face to face?

Janet: Actually, I'm quite busy. Perhaps you could send me your CV and a cover letter and I'll have a look at it.

Eryk: I will do that. Thank you very much for your time. I hope to hear from you soon.

Janet: Thanks for your call.

2.1

Silvia: So, Sophie, I've found a really interesting-looking job vacancy at a communications agency in central London.

Sophie: That's great. Have you sent off your application?

Silvia: Actually, you were so great at helping me work out what my skills were, I was wondering if you could give me some words of wisdom on writing a killer CV.

Sophie: Of course. Okay, so the two most popular ways of organising a CV are a conventional chronological CV and a skills-based CV.

Silvia: Okay.

Sophie: So, obviously both of them start with your name in large letters.

Silvia: Why large?

Sophie: Your name's got to be large so that the interviewer can easily find your CV hidden away in a pile of papers on their desk when they interview you! Then after that come your contact details: address, telephone number, email address and so on. Oh, and make sure it's a sensible email address, your name@hotmail.com, for example.

Silvia: Okay.

Sophie: If you were going to include a personal statement then it would go before this bit under your contact details, but they're a lot more common in skills-based CVs. So, in a chronological CV you'd start with an education section, outlining your main academic qualifications, most recent first. As well as the basics – university name, degree and graduation date – you can include coursework that's relevant to the job, academic honours or awards.

Silvia: Then what?

Sophie: Then you'd put your work experience next in chronological order starting with the most recent, with dates, duties, and the key skills you gained in each position.

Silvia: What about my expedition in Argentina last year? Where would I put that?

Sophie: Well, after your education section and work experience in a traditional chronological CV, you'd have a section on activities and interests – I'd put it in there. But remember to focus on the skills relevant for the job that these activities and interests helped you to develop.

Silvia: Right.

Sophie: And then lastly, you can list additional skills such as languages, computer skills, clean driving licence and so on. It depends on the job really, and who's applying.

Silvia: What do you mean?

Sophie: Well, just include the things that are relevant for the job. If you were a writer, for example, you might list your publications here. Whereas if you worked in computers, you'd have a specific section focusing on your computer skills.

Silvia: I see. And then at the bottom I put my references?

Sophie: Exactly.

Silvia: So what's the difference with a skills-based CV then?

Sophie: Well, with a skills-based CV you'd start the same, but then it's quite different. Some people include a personal statement or career profile. It's just a couple of sentences that summarise your value to the employer. It's not a bad idea to write one even if you decide not to use it, as just writing one will help you decide how you want to present yourself and what you want out of your career.

Silvia: Good idea. I'll give it a go.

Sophie: Okay, then after that in a skills-based CV you list your key skills. Basically, you decide what transferable skills the employer is looking for, and then you break these down into similar groups and provide evidence that you've got these skills.

Silvia: So you mean when the job advertisement mentions that they are looking for somebody who's 'an excellent communicator' and has 'great research skills', I should write the CV directly in reaction to that, with skills headings, such as 'Communication', 'Research' and so on?

Sophie: Yes. That's it. This approach is quite effective as it focuses your CV towards a specific job and proves you've got all the skills they're after. Then after that you simply list your work experience details, education and professional qualifications, interests and lastly your referees.

Silvia: I quite like the sound of a skills-based CV, but I think the chronological CV seems easier to write.

Sophie: It is. And remember these are just two approaches. There aren't really any strict rules on what order to put your sections in, or even what you want to call these sections. As long as the essential information is there, it's up to you. It's your CV and how you design and create it says something about you and reflects your character.

Silvia: Thanks, I'm really inspired now.

2.2

Alex: Hi, Ella.

Ella: Hi, Alex. How are you doing?

Alex: I'm fine. I'm just calling as I've decided to apply for a couple of admin jobs, and I'd like your help with my CV. Do you have any tips? Any specific mistakes I should watch out for?

Ella: Well, the first one is simply mistakes. You'd be surprised how many people submit CVs with basic mistakes in them. If you've got a whole load of CVs on your desk, this is an easy way to get rid of some to begin with.

Alex: What sort of mistakes are you talking about?

Ella: Spelling mistakes, often. For example, putting the 'i' in the wrong place in 'receive', or writing 'correspondence' with an 'a' instead of an 'e', or spelling 'liaise' with only one 'i'. Then there's another type of spelling mistake, when applicants use the wrong form of words like 'practice' and 'advice'.

Alex: English is such a difficult language sometimes! I guess the answer is to proofread my CV thoroughly and then double and triple check.

Ella: Exactly. The next thing is to keep it short. You've got to grab the employer's attention, and remember they've got other work to do as well as going through CVs. Don't list all of your experience and qualifications, only the stuff that's relevant for the job you're going for. Cut it down to the most relevant and impressive achievements. Less is more, and being concise and to the point will demonstrate your ability to edit well.

Alex: So how many pages should it be?

Ella: Well, I'd aim for one side if possible, certainly nothing longer than two pages.

Alex: That's great. Anything else?

Ella: Yes, be honest.

Alex: But doesn't everyone lie a bit in their CVs?

Ella: It's true that a lot of people stretch the truth, and you should certainly only focus on positive experience and details relevant for the job, but don't be tempted to write anything untrue. First of all, your CV is a legal document, and if they find out you've lied then they can fire you just like that. Secondly, you're going to be a lot more confident in an interview talking about the details on your CV if you've told the truth, than if you've made something up. In my experience it doesn't take very long to spot someone who's lied in their CV and they always get found out sooner or later. It's simply not worth it.

Alex: So honesty is the best policy. And what about getting my CV noticed?

Ella: Well, presentation's important so use nice, neutral-coloured paper and matching envelope. But I think the main thing is to make sure that your CV is written to match the requirements of the job and the culture of the company you're applying for work with. You've got to adapt every CV you write to each job you apply for. It's surprising how many people think they can get away with one CV for all jobs!

Alex: Thanks, Ella. I can't thank you enough.

Ella: You're welcome, Alex. Let me know how you get on.

▇ 2.3

Klaudia: Thanks for proofreading my CV, Tom. What did you think?

Tom: Well, your work experience section is a bit thin. It doesn't really tell us much.

Klaudia: That's because I've only had one proper job. And I'm only a secretary, so there's not really anything impressive to say.

Tom: Oh, I don't know. What do you actually do in your job?

Klaudia: Boring things like answering the phone, filling in forms, taking minutes …

Tom: Hang on a sec. Answering the phone? So you deal with customers? You represent your company, you represent your boss. Who is your boss?

Klaudia: She's the managing director.

Tom: It sounds like you're more of a PA than a secretary. Listen, just the fact that you are trusted by the managing director to manage her affairs is impressive. Lots of people wouldn't be able to work at such a high level.

Klaudia: But I don't do anything clever. It's just basic stuff.

Tom: I wouldn't know how to do what you do. The fact that you find it easy means you're intelligent, quick to learn, hard-working …

Klaudia: Hmm, maybe. But should I mention all that on my CV?

Tom: Absolutely. You need to select the most important things, the most relevant things for the job you're applying for. What is the job, by the way?

Klaudia: It's an executive PA job for an international bank.

Tom: So quite high-powered then? Did you say you take minutes at meetings?

Klaudia: Yes, at board meetings.

Tom: Don't you think that's impressive? It shows you can follow high-level meetings, listen and write intelligently, and produce important and reliable company documents. I'd say that's pretty impressive.

Klaudia: I suppose so.

Tom: And what about before? You've never done any other job?

Klaudia: Only casual jobs. Nothing special. When I was in New York I worked as a nanny for three months.

Tom: In New York? You didn't mention that on your resume! That's really impressive – if you've lived and worked abroad, you've got to mention it. Where else have you worked?

Klaudia: Well, I spent one summer in Madrid, but I was only working in a restaurant. I was a waitress. Actually, when I first got to Madrid, I spent a few weeks cleaning hotel rooms. It was disgusting.

Tom: So you speak Spanish?

Klaudia: Not really, just enough to get by.

Tom: Sounds like you had enough to get a job, two jobs in fact. And to deal with customers in the language. All of this is really great. You've got to mention it on your resume. Your nannying job shows you're responsible, and reminds us of your excellent English. Even your cleaning job tells us a lot about your character – you're not afraid to get your hands dirty, you're flexible and hard-working. These are the kinds of life experiences that employers love to hear about.

Klaudia: So you think I should mention them?

Tom: Yes, of course. But you've got to focus on all those points that I mentioned. Right, pass me your pen …

▇ 2.4

Oliver: What do you call this section on your CV? I usually tell people to keep it simple and call it 'interests', which generally covers everything.

Grace: I think that's fine. Some people put 'personal interests'. I don't think it matters too much what the section is labelled as long as the contents make the potential employer more interested in you.

Oliver: Yes, employers are obviously keen to check you have the skills and experience necessary to do the job, but they also want to know a bit more about you to see if you're going to fit in with the rest of the company. This section is an insight into your personality.

Grace: Yes, after all, the V in CV stands for *vitae*, which is Latin for 'life', so the interests section is about demonstrating that you have a life! Still, why is it that candidates often make such a mess of this section and fail to take advantage of it?

Oliver: I think it's partly to do with the fact that we're generally not very good at writing about interests and free-time activities; we find it a bit embarrassing. This is made even worse when we don't think about these activities in terms of the skills we need to complete them. If everybody did that, then you'd start seeing a lot more impressive interests sections in CVs.

Grace: So you mean I'd get more than simply reading, going to the theatre and football?

Oliver: Yes. I think so.

Grace: I mean, 'football' – this doesn't even tell us if the applicant plays football or just enjoys sitting in front of the television watching their favourite team.

Oliver: I agree. If your interests are active, and it's better to include active interests than passive ones, then it's worth highlighting this fact. Most job-hunters simply do not go into enough detail in this section. Where they could be demonstrating their personality, their skills and achievements, they come across as dull and uninteresting. For example, I once read a CV where under the interests section the applicant had just written, 'captain of the football team'. Okay, being a captain is an achievement but it doesn't really tell us that much. Was he a good captain, or a bad one? I later found out that he had led his team through a competitive university competition, and had motivated the team to their first year appearance in the final. Why didn't he put some of that in his CV? It would've made such a difference and been so much more impressive.

Grace: Yes, different sports can suggest all sorts of skills and abilities, as well as the obvious one, that you keep fit. I mean, why make an unsubstantiated claim like 'I work well in teams' if you can demonstrate it by telling the employer you play volleyball for your university?

Oliver: It's not just sports though. There are all sorts of things you can list.

Grace: Yes, and a wide range of interests always looks good because the employer will want to see that you can fit into different environments easily.

Oliver: Basically, I'd say the main thing is to avoid dull lists and offer a variety of interests. With each example it's the specific details that make it interesting to the reader and that will give you something concrete to talk about if you get to the interview stage.

Grace: That's very true. I'd only add that as well as giving examples, you should emphasise any achievements related to your interests.

Oliver: So, Grace, what would you put under interests then?

Grace: I usually stick with my ability to pick up foreign languages quickly, and that I'm a member of an orchestra. But at the moment I'm raising sponsorship to do the London Marathon in April. I've got to raise £1900, all of which goes to charity. If I manage to raise the money and get through the 26 miles on the day then I'm definitely going to add it to my CV!

Oliver: Well, best of luck. I'll sponsor you if you like.

Grace: That'd be great.

▇ 2.5

Grace: So, Oliver, who would you choose to act as a referee on your CV?

Oliver: Well, it's quite a long time since I went to university, so I wouldn't put my old personal tutor – I haven't spoken to her in years. For me, I'd have to go with two professional referees, one from my last job and one from the one I've got at the minute, as long as I knew that my current boss wouldn't be contacted until later in the application process.

Grace: Yes, that could potentially be extremely awkward, couldn't it? What about friends who know you well?

Oliver: I'd say it's better to go with a professional or academic referee than friends. The way I see it, friends can only really provide a character reference and are not usually in a position to comment on your performance at work.

Grace: Yes, I agree, I think it's better to resist the temptation of putting a friend, even though you know they will sing your praises. Recent graduates should definitely have an academic referee.

Oliver: Yeah, a personal tutor or the head of the course or any of the lecturers that they got on well with.

Grace: Exactly. An academic reference can be really useful if you didn't get the results you were expecting, as they can confirm the reasons for this – if you were ill, for example. In that way a bad result might not actually harm your chances of getting a job.

Oliver: That's a good point.

Grace: Basically, I think employers contact referees to confirm the facts on your CV, and so long as your referees can back up the facts, then you've got nothing to worry about.

Oliver: Well, yes, but you also want your referees to say lots of nice things about you. Another important thing is to give a copy of your CV to your referee, which will then help them when they're asked to provide a reference.

Grace: Yeah, you're right. It's amazing how many people forget to do this. And then all you've got to do is add the names and contact details to the end of your CV.

Oliver: Well, actually no. I'm not so sure I agree with you on this one.

Grace: What do you mean?

Oliver: In my opinion you don't need to provide the names and contact details of your references in your CV. I think it's a waste of valuable space, especially if you're trying to get your CV on a single page.

Grace: But how will your employer contact your referees?

Oliver: Well, that's just it. I don't think at this stage of the application process that they're going to. You can simply put 'References available on request' and then provide them later on if you're asked to. The aim of the CV is to get you an interview, and I don't think any employer is going to spend their valuable time checking references before they've even met you and think you could be the right person for the job.

Grace: Hmm, I hadn't really thought of it like that.

Oliver: Plus, if you were planning to change jobs, this would solve the potential problem of your current boss being contacted by the company you're applying for work with.

Grace: I can see your point. But what if I've got a really impressive referee? Someone who's going to impress the potential future employer?

Oliver: Well, in that case I'd certainly think about including them, if I had enough space.

3.1

Felix: Hello, Felix speaking.

Vicky: Hi, Felix. It's Vicky.

Felix: Hi, Vicky. It's good to hear from you. What can I do for you?

Vicky: I'm after a bit of career advice, actually.

Felix: Really? Are you changing jobs?

Vicky: Hopefully, yes. I've been working for Green Pharmaceuticals for three years now, but I feel my career prospects here are rather limited. Anyway, I've found a couple of interesting jobs online.

Felix: I see. So have you applied for any of the jobs?

Vicky: Not yet, no. I haven't written a cover letter for years and I'm not really sure what to put in it. I wondered whether you've got any tips or suggestions that could help?

3.2

Felix: Cover letters are really important, and I've got some great tips that I give all job seekers.

Vicky: Oh thanks, Felix.

Felix: First of all, it's extremely important that you create a positive impression. If you're sending your application by post then you should use good-quality, matching paper for your cover letter and CV.

Vicky: Right.

Felix: Also, remember not to be too informal as you want to sound as professional as possible. So don't use any contractions – you know, write 'I am' and not 'I'm', for example.

Vicky: Okay.

Felix: Right. The most important thing to bear in mind is that every cover letter should be written specifically for the position you're applying for. You should show that you've read about the company, done some research and thought about the specific position you're applying for.

Vicky: What, you mean I should investigate the company in more depth, on the Internet for example?

Felix: Exactly. Find out as much as you possibly can. Then, when you write your letter, you should concentrate on demonstrating the skills that are required for the post, what you can offer the company.

Vicky: I see what you mean. Do you think I should send a copy of my university degree certificate with the letter?

Felix: No, don't bother. If a company wants to see any documents like that, they'll ask for them later. I'll tell you what. I'll send you a copy of a really good cover letter and make some notes on it so you can see what I mean and use it for inspiration.

Vicky: Thanks so much, Felix, you've been a great help. I'll let you know how I get on with the application.

Felix: No problem. And if you need anything else, just ask.

3.3

Oliver: Well, Grace, what do you think about this as an opening for a cover letter?

Grace: I'm sorry to say, but I think it's a bit of a disaster, Oliver. First of all, the applicant hasn't even mentioned what position they're applying for, and in the second sentence they have obviously just taken a lot of phrases straight from the company's own website, word for word.

Oliver: Yes, I see what you mean. It's really important that the applicant makes it immediately clear precisely what job they're applying for. This example is far too vague. And when it comes to company phrases and mission statements, it'd be much better if the applicant had put this into their own words.

Grace: I totally agree.

Oliver: Now this next cover letter is much better. The applicant has specifically mentioned the position they're applying for and also how they found out about the job.

Grace: You're right, but later on at the end of the paragraph the applicant claims that they're the right person for the job just because they are interested in the position.

Oliver: I know!

Grace: It simply isn't logical to say that you're suitable for a job because you're interested in it. I'm interested in medicine but I'm certainly not qualified to be a doctor. The applicant should've concentrated more on how their academic background matches the requirements for the job.

Oliver: What do you think about the last example?

Grace: It starts off okay but the ending is far too confident and boastful for me.

Oliver: Definitely. The applicant should have toned down the phrase 'have absolutely no doubt' – it's far too strong. A better alternative would be 'I am confident that' or 'I believe that'.

Grace: Yes. I also think that 'an indispensable member' is too strong. I'd prefer something like 'a valuable asset' or 'a competent candidate'. They could have even rephrased the sentence slightly and finished with 'I believe

this experience has provided me with the qualifications, experience and skills you are looking for.'

Oliver: Yes, I like that.

3.4

Grace: What do you think of the ending to this cover letter, Oliver?

Oliver: Well, I like the phrase 'I would appreciate the opportunity to meet with you to discuss my credentials' – it's very polite and professional. But I'm not so keen on the first line. Very few applicants can boast about having too much experience or too many skills to cover in their letter. I think this is best avoided.

Grace: Yes, I agree with that. There are definitely too many letters in which applicants make amazing claims without having any evidence to back them up. What about the other example?

Oliver: I like it. It's a good ending for me. The tone is appropriate, it's tentative and polite. Especially the use of 'might' in the phrase 'how I might contribute to your company'.

Grace: Yes. It's certainly positive. The only thing I'd add is that, although it's good that the applicant has mentioned the company's goals, it's important that they really have a good understanding of what these goals are. Otherwise it's going to be very difficult for them to explain how they are going to help the company fulfil them when they're invited to an interview.

Oliver: You're right. That's a good point. I also like the fact that the applicant has thanked the company for their time and consideration.

Grace: Yeah. It's very polite and respectful.

4.1

Nina: Hi, Silvia. I understand that you are preparing for an interview.

Silvia: Yes, my interview is next week and I'm already really nervous.

Nina: Okay. So, let's start at the beginning. Do you know where the office is?

Silvia: No.

Nina: Well, you need to make sure you know exactly where you're going. I would suggest that you arrive at the office at least ten minutes early so that you can enter the company exactly on time. Take an umbrella in case it rains, and make sure you've got a contact telephone number so that you can call if you get delayed on the way.

Silvia: That's a great idea. I was also going to ask my friend, Jill, to give me a lift and come along for some support on the day. I thought I'd meet up with her to practise my English before the interview as it's going to be the first time I've ever had an interview in English!

Nina: It's a good idea to meet a friend to practise your English before the interview, to get you warmed up if you like, but I wouldn't take anyone into the building itself.

Silvia: Oh. Why not?

Nina: You want to demonstrate your independence, and you'll only do this by arriving on time on your own and appearing relaxed. Another thing you should do is take a copy of your resume and examples of your work with you.

Silvia: But I've already sent them to the company.

Nina: Yes, I know. But there's no reason why you can't take extra copies for yourself, and anyway they might not be able to find yours. Most candidates don't do this, so it'll impress the interviewer and show them that you're well-organised. During the interview it's almost certain that the interviewer will refer to things written on your resume. Having a copy of your own will help you to organise a successful response.

Silvia: What tips have you got on answering questions?

Nina: Well, obviously there are some questions that you can predict you're going to be asked during the interview. Some questions always come up, and others you know you'll be asked because of what's on your resume, or simply because of the job you've applied for. You should definitely spend some time thinking about how you might answer these questions, and learn some impressive words and phrases in English to use at the interview. However, I don't think it's a great idea to memorise long answers, as you'll seem mechanical and unnatural.

Silvia: So you think I should practise some expressions in English, but I shouldn't try to memorise complete answers?

Nina: Exactly.

Silvia: And what about what I should wear for the interview? It's for a communications agency in central London.

Nina: Well, I would definitely suggest wearing smart, formal clothes, especially if it's a job dealing with clients or customers. And it's better to tie or comb your hair back.

Silvia: Why's that?

Nina: Making sure your hair isn't covering your eyes demonstrates openness and suggests you have nothing to hide.

Silvia: How interesting. I'd never thought of it like that.

Nina: Oh, one last thing.

Silvia: Yes?

Nina: Do you use any of those social networking sites, like Facebook, for example?

Silvia: Yeah! I use Facebook all the time.

Nina: Employers often check applicants out on sites like these. It's pretty much common practice for big City firms.

Silvia: Really? How scary!

Nina: Exactly. So check your privacy settings so that you can control who has access to your page. And check the content of your site so that whatever information they do see will help you come across as a professional individual and exactly the type of person they'd like to employ.

Silvia: That's a great idea. Thanks, Nina. You've been a real help.

4.2

1

Silvia: Hello. I'm here for an interview with Mr Lewis. My name is Silvia Carnali.

Receptionist: Ah yes, Ms Carnali. Nice to meet you. I'm afraid Mr Lewis is in a meeting at the moment.

Silvia: That's quite all right. Shall I take a seat and wait over there?

Receptionist: Yes, I'm sure he'll be out in a minute. Can I get you anything while you wait?

Silvia: No, thank you, I'm fine. Actually, have you got a company brochure or something I could read about the company?

Receptionist: Yes, of course. Here's a recent company brochure.

Silvia: That's great. Thank you very much. By the way, do you know how many people are being interviewed for this job?

Receptionist: As far as I know, there's only two of you scheduled for today, although I think there might be another candidate tomorrow morning. That's it, I think.

Matt Lewis: Hello. You must be Silvia Carnali. I'm Matt Lewis.

Silvia: Yes, that's right. It's a pleasure to meet you.

Matt: I'm sorry I'm late. Our meeting overran a bit.

Silvia: That's okay. I was just admiring the office.

Matt: So, Silvia – may I call you Silvia?

Silvia: Of course.

Matt: How are you?

Silvia: I'm very well, thank you.

Matt: Would you like a coffee or a drink before we begin?

Silvia: No, thank you, I'm fine.

Matt: Okay. Well, let's go into my office then, shall we?

2

Karl: Good morning. My name is Karl Osborne. I'm Head of Production here at the theatre. It's nice to meet you at last.

Alex: Thank you. It's nice to meet you too, Mr Osborne.

Karl: Please, call me Karl.

Alex: Thank you. And I'm Alex.

Karl: So, Alex. Did you have any trouble finding us?

Alex: No, no trouble at all. Your directions were excellent.

Karl: How did you get here?

Alex: Well, I got the train to Liverpool Street and then I got the tube.

Karl: So you managed to avoid the rain then? I can't believe the weather at the moment!

Alex: I know. It's awful, isn't it? Still, it's supposed to get better by the weekend.

Karl: Let's hope so. So, Alex, how did you find out about us? We're quite a small theatre and we didn't advertise the position in a lot of places.

Alex: You were highly recommended to me by a friend who works here. He heard about the job and suggested I apply.

Karl: Oh really, who was that?

4.3

1

I remember the first interview I ever had for a traineeship in the City. I had difficulty finding the company and had to run to the interview to avoid being late. I arrived covered in sweat. I must've looked and smelt terrible. It's enough to say that I didn't get the position. My advice would be to find out where the office is before the interview to avoid being late, and to use a good deodorant before going in.

2

I used to be extremely nervous during interviews. There was this one time when there was a panel of three interviewers rather than just one. I was almost sick when I walked in the door. My voice started shaking throughout the interview. I thought I was going to have a panic attack. I've slowly learnt to overcome this problem. I try to think positively and confidently and relax. I take a couple of big deep breaths before I go in and then during the interview concentrate on breathing slowly and taking my time to answer the questions as calmly as I can.

3

After four unsuccessful interviews I decided to start practising my technique with a friend to try and discover what was going wrong. Immediately my friend helped me to identify the problem. When I was answering the questions I had a tendency to look at the floor and not back into the interviewer's eyes. It was really obvious as soon as I realised what I'd been doing. Now I make a real effort to look into the interviewer's eyes, taking care not to stare, though. It's worked for me.

4

In my first interview, not wanting to seem scared or nervous, I leaned back in the chair as I thought it would make me seem more relaxed. It was a terrible mistake. I must've looked like a lazy teenager watching TV. In my current job I interview people on a regular basis and my advice would be that it's important to sit up straight during the interview, with your hands either on your lap or on the arm of the chair. When you answer questions it's also a good idea to lean slightly forward and then lean back when you've finished speaking. This will help the flow of the interview as the interviewer will realise when you've finished.

5

The last interview I had was for a secretarial position with a big international accountancy firm. I really wanted the job and was very excited and nervous about the interview. Right at the beginning of the interview, the interviewer offered me a coffee. I was so nervous that my hands started shaking uncontrollably and I spilled it all over myself. I was so embarrassed. I got cleaned up and then had the interview, still smelling of coffee. Amazingly I still got the job. I'm sure they must've just felt sorry for me. But my advice would be never accept any drinks during an interview, except possibly a glass of water, as there is far too great a risk of disaster, especially if your hands shake like mine do. Play it safe and refuse the offer politely.

4.4

1

Well, I've never really thought about it. I suppose I'd like to be married with kids, perhaps. My sister's got three kids, and they're really great. I'd also like to be doing a job I enjoy. There's nothing worse than being stuck in a boring job where you have the same routine every day. It'd be a job with lots of responsibility, but I suppose not too much. I wouldn't want to get stressed. If I was lucky enough to get this job, it'd be great, but I suppose five years is a long time without a change, so I'd try to get a promotion, if I could.

2

They'd say I was a great leader and an essential member of any team. They'd say my judgement was inspired, and that I rarely make any mistakes.

3

Well, usually there needs to be a clear picture of what the aims of the project are. So it's essential to speak to everyone involved before taking any action. In my current job we use project management software to help us keep track of what we have to do and when we have to do it. Of course, it's important that someone keeps an eye on whether people are actually doing what they're supposed to be doing, and obviously you also need to deal with unexpected situations as they come up.

4.5

I see myself doing a job I really enjoy. I'll have plenty of responsibility, which will make me proud of the work I do. But I won't be stressed, because I'll make sure I only take on what I can manage. If you offer me this job, I'll expect to impress you enough with my attitude and my results that you'll offer me a promotion.

4.6

The first thing I do is make sure I've got a really clear picture of what I need to achieve. Let me give you an example. Last year I managed a project to archive all our old customer billing records, which were in huge piles of paper in a storage room. So I needed to be really clear about what information was important. I always speak to everyone involved before I take any action. In this case, I spoke to the admin staff who were actually going to use the archive, as well as to their boss, to find out what they needed. I always use project management software to help me keep track of what I have to do and when I have to do it. This was really important with my archiving project, because I was managing quite a large team of people. But I also make sure I keep an eye on whether my team are actually doing what they're supposed to be doing, and don't just rely on the software. And I deal with unexpected situations as they come up. For example, several members of my team went on sick leave, and I had to get some temporary workers in and train them up quickly so I didn't miss any deadlines.

4.7

Interviewer: Can you tell us something about yourself?

Alejandro: Well, I'm 24. I recently graduated from the University of Barcelona with a BSc in Economics. I enjoy playing sports, especially tennis and basketball. Our basketball team got to the regional final in my last year at university.

Interviewer: What did you learn during your time at university?

Alejandro: I studied Economics. And, well, I learnt a lot about economics, microeconomics, macroeconomics, positive economics, and how economies work as economic systems, and what the relationship is between economic players in society.

Interviewer: What kinds of things do you worry about?

Alejandro: I worry about quite a lot of things. I worry about the environment. I worry about my work. My work is extremely important and I can be a perfectionist at times, everything has to be just right. If there's something wrong with a project I'm working on, then I can get really frustrated and worried until it's sorted out. I had a problem like this last week, but it was okay in the end. I also worry about catching tropical diseases when I go on holiday.

Interviewer: Would you say you're an ambitious person?

Alejandro: Yes, I would say that I'm ambitious. Definitely.

4.8

Grace: The first question was 'tell us something about yourself'. Here Alejandro makes two major mistakes. Firstly, his response is too short – all your answers should be between 20 seconds and two minutes. Secondly, he has made the common mistake of simply repeating details from his CV. You should use this opportunity to demonstrate your skills and experience relevant for the post you are being interviewed for.

Now his second answer about what he learnt at university sounds impressive, but it's a bit confusing. It feels like Alejandro has just listed some of the options on his degree course and he doesn't demonstrate that he has learnt anything. He doesn't go into enough detail or relate his answer to the requirements of the position. With this question I think the employer is really interested in real-life transferable skills that Alejandro will be able to use in the position he has applied for.

When Alejandro starts talking about the kinds of things he worries about I think the interviewer would really start to get a bit worried at this point! His answer about work is okay but he goes on far too long. I think he mentioned the environment to sound serious but he didn't go into any detail, and his fear of tropical diseases, well, that's not something I'd share in an interview! If I were Alejandro, I'd stick to common professional concerns and keep my answer brief.

The question about whether Alejandro is an ambitious person is an excellent opportunity to talk about career plans which include your prospective employer. Don't mention any professional objectives if they don't include the organisation that is interviewing you. It's best to talk about how you are looking forward to developing a lasting relationship with the company interviewing you.

4.9

Interviewer: Can you tell us something about yourself?

Alejandro: Well, I'm motivated and I put a lot of effort into everything I do, whether I'm studying at university, at work or even when I'm playing sport. During my last year at university I was captain of the basketball team. I had to organise matches and motivate the players. As captain it was essential that I was able to communicate effectively and get along with everybody in the team … and for the first time in years our team managed to reach the regional final. We didn't win, unfortunately, but leading the team to the final was a big achievement for me.

Interviewer: What did you learn during your time at university?

Alejandro: Oh, lots of things. My Economics degree was very practical, and there were many elements of the degree that could be applied to the business world. I had a number of challenging assignments, which often had to be completed within a short period of time. This helped me to develop my prioritising skills and ability to work to tight deadlines.

Interviewer: What kinds of things do you worry about?

Alejandro: I worry about normal things, the same as everybody else, I think. I worry about meeting deadlines and getting everything done on time. I used to worry about data on my computer quite a bit. Now I back up all my data on an external hard drive, so that everything is protected. This way I've got one less thing to worry about.

Interviewer: Would you say you're an ambitious person?

Alejandro: Yes, I would say that I'm ambitious. I'm very keen to get a job with a company such as yours where I can make full use of my degree and professional experience. I am a dedicated worker and would hope to gain internal promotion based on my performance at work.

4.10

Grace: 'What do you see as your strengths?' This is such a common question and so often it's wasted! It's a golden opportunity to concentrate on your strengths and why you are the right candidate for the post.

Oliver: I agree. Although it's not a good idea just to claim that you're really good at certain things without also giving some evidence to prove that these claims are true. Applicants need to use evidence from their experience to support what they say.

Grace: I think it's also important that they use confident, direct language, such as 'I am good at' rather than using weaker, tentative language like 'Well, I think I'm quite good at'.

Oliver: Right. An interview is not a time to be modest about your strengths and abilities. You've got to sell yourself. How about 'What university did you attend and why did you choose it?'

Grace: I chose my university as it was the closest to home!

Oliver: But you wouldn't say that in an interview, would you?

Grace: No, not at all. With this question the university that someone chooses isn't as important as their reasons for selecting it. The question is assessing an applicant's reasoning ability. So, you should focus on the academic and educational reasons involved in your decision. For example, 'I chose to go to this university because it had a good English department'.

Oliver: Exactly. I'd also stress that the decision was your own and not your parents'.

Grace: 'What are your weaknesses?' What do you think of applicants that say they have no weaknesses?

Oliver: Well, I'd think that they're lying or completely lacking any sort of self-awareness.

Grace: I would use this question to give a weakness that could be perceived as a strength, such as 'I can be a bit of a perfectionist'. Although I would avoid personal characteristics that could be perceived as serious character flaws.

Oliver: Hmm. I'm not sure I agree. I would state a knowledge-based weakness, for example needing to improve IT skills, and then go on to talk about the things you are doing to remedy this problem. Now, what about 'What do you like doing in your spare time?'

Grace: Ah. What interviewers are looking for here are your transferable skills.

Oliver: Yes, exactly. So somebody who likes team sports is likely to be better at working in a team, whereas individual sports might indicate determination and self-motivation. Saying that you play chess suggests intelligence and analytical skills.

Grace: Right. I think the best advice here is to be specific and try to include something unusual, as this will raise the interviewer's interests and help them to remember you over other candidates. It's a shame that so many applicants just say something general such as travelling or reading.

Oliver: I agree. If they are going to say that, they should at least be specific and talk about places they've travelled to, and the types of books they enjoy reading. Also, it's great if you can identify interests that share characteristics with the requirements for the job. This would obviously impress any interviewer.

Grace: That's a great piece of advice.

🔲 4.11

Interviewer: What do you see as your strengths?

Lidia: I am organised and apply a systematic approach to my work. I believe in good time management. This enables me to get work done in time. I'm also able to prioritise my work and work under pressure if deadlines are moved forward. For example, in my last job there were quieter periods and periods of high activity when there was a lot of pressure to complete tasks on time. I implemented a new system for managing the workload in our team and planning ahead. This way we were able to share the work more effectively and always ensure that we had the capacity to deal with increased pressure and any unexpected problems.

Rafa: Well, that's a difficult question to answer. I think I'm a very hard worker and somebody who takes pride in my work. Being very determined means that I always make sure that I complete work that I set myself. I'm reliable and good at working with other people. I can speak French and Spanish fluently and definitely feel I have the skills that this job requires.

Interviewer: What university did you attend and why did you choose it?

Lidia: I did a lot of research into universities, both abroad and in Spain. In the end I decided to go to the University of Barcelona as it was clear that its Economics department had an excellent reputation. I'm also interested in doing an International MBA at the Instituto de Empresa in Madrid in the future.

Rafa: Well, I wasn't sure to be honest but Sevilla university was the easiest option as it was closest, and also my parents really wanted me to go there.

Interviewer: What are your weaknesses?

Lidia: Well, my French is a bit rusty, so I have recently started evening classes to improve it. I used to be a bit disorganised at university but I've started using to-do lists, which has enabled me to prioritise tasks more efficiently.

Rafa: That's a difficult question. I'd have to say that my main weaknesses are that I am a perfectionist and insist on everything being just right, and that I am quite stubborn at times.

Interviewer: What do you like doing in your spare time?

Lidia: I enjoy playing volleyball and was captain of the team during my last year at university. I still play regularly for a local club and love going away with the team for matches against other clubs. I'm also a keen traveller. During the summer last year I spent a month in Africa working with volunteers at a national reserve. I'm currently planning an expedition to Thailand.

Rafa: In my free time I enjoy reading, going to the cinema, travelling and I also go swimming twice a week.

🔲 4.12

Matt: What do you know about Futerra and why would you like to work here?

Silvia: Well, before applying for this position I did some research into the market and Futerra came out on top. I know that Futerra is a small organisation, which is just what I'm looking for. I had a look at your website and could see that you work with a variety of people, from informing journalists about climate change to developing communication strategies for NGOs, businesses and the government. This impressed me a lot.

Dan: That's great to hear, but can you tell us why this impressed you?

Silvia: Well, it's really something that attracted me to Futerra. The fact that you work with lots of different clients in various sectors means there would probably be a variety of interesting and different projects to get involved in.

Matt: That's true. And what attracted you to the position of Junior Consultant?

Silvia: Well, one of my strengths is developing communication strategies, and I've been looking for an organisation that does a lot of communication and marketing work, as well as dealing with environmental issues. Basically, I'd like a position where I could use my communication experience on projects that personally appeal to me. The Junior Consultant post combines these two areas at a company with a well-established reputation.

Matt: You mentioned that you looked at our website. What did you think of it?

Silvia: I thought it was very attractive and professional, really excellent. You came across online as an exciting, dynamic place to work. It's clear from your website that Futerra is quite a small company, which means that everybody has got to work well as a team, with everybody playing an important role.

Dan: Wouldn't you prefer to work for a bigger organisation?

Silvia: No. I would rather work in this sort of environment where the impact of your work is clearer and more immediate, than work for a huge multinational company where I think I'd feel lost, a tiny part of a huge machine. I definitely feel, from everything I've learnt about Futerra, that this is the type of organisation I'd like to work for.

🔲 4.13

Matt: Well, Dan, what did you think of her?

Dan: I liked her. She'd certainly done her homework on us. I mean, I was very impressed when she said that before applying for the position she'd done a lot of research into the market and that we had come out on top. It was clear that she'd really looked hard at our website.

Matt: Yes, I agree.

Dan: I think she's the first candidate that knew that we work with a wide variety of clients, and had identified who these clients were.

Matt: That's true. I also liked the fact that she was confident and supported her claim that she understood the issues we deal with. I came away feeling that she really does understand a lot about sustainability.

Dan: Yes, and her recent work experience and knowledge from her MSc definitely fit in with what we're looking for. Lots of applicants have looked great on paper, but she really seemed to know what we're about and what the job here would involve.

🔲 4.14

Interviewer: What skills and experiences do you have that are relevant for this position?

Susana: I think the position of sales assistant requires somebody who has got good customer service skills. In my last job at Alton Towers Themepark I was responsible for selling souvenirs, so I am used to dealing with customers. Initially I was only responsible for operating various rides, but as I can speak both Italian and English fluently, and have a good command of French, I was asked to work in the gift shop instead. This period of employment also gave me valuable experience of managing people, as after two weeks in the shop I was

promoted to senior sales assistant, where I managed two other employees. When I was at university in Turin, before moving to England last summer, I used to be the captain of the female volleyball team, which included managing the team and also the finances for playing fees. I think the leadership skills that I have developed both at university and in my last job are very relevant for this position. So, to sum up, I feel I am a highly effective communicator, fluent in Italian and English and very proficient in French. I can work well under pressure and am able to delegate effectively. Having worked with a variety of different teams I would say I have a proven track record in teamwork.

🔲 4.15

Dan: How do your skills and experience match the requirements for the position of Junior Consultant at Futerra?

Silvia: Well, I think I'm suitable for the position at Futerra because I understand the issues you deal with and am passionate about them. Four years ago I joined Greenpeace and have been an active member ever since. Following my BA I found out about an exciting project in Kenya and spent six months there educating local people about the need for reforestation. That's really when I started getting interested in sustainability and also when I started learning about different communication strategies. For example, our team found that simply putting up posters didn't really have much of an impact, but going and talking to respected members of the community and getting them to talk to others was much more effective. When I was at university I was the communications officer of the student union and I was responsible for dealing with suppliers and other student organisations. So I've got quite a lot of communication experience. I know you're also looking for someone who's good at research. For my dissertation for my MA I'm researching how best to communicate reforestation issues, building on my own practical experiences gained in Kenya. So to sum up, I think I'm suitable for the position at Futerra for three reasons. Firstly, I've done a lot of communication work. Secondly, I'm a good team worker, and finally, because I have a good understanding of the sustainability issues this agency deals with.

🔲 5.1

1

Well, during my studies I used to support myself by working part-time in a law office. Most of the time it worked well. I could manage my time so that I could work when I didn't have lectures. Also, it really helped me with my studies to have some real-life experience to support the theoretical input I was getting at university. But then in my final year, I was offered the chance to get involved in a really high-powered case with a major multinational client who wanted to take over a local company. I was very keen to get involved because it was exactly the sort of experience I needed. The problem was, it was at exactly the same time as my exam session. I had to choose between studying for my exams and getting involved in the case ...

2

A few years ago my college got involved in a competition against other colleges to design and build innovative labour-saving devices. It was just a bit of fun, but the idea was that we'd develop our practical design and engineering skills as well as our ability to cooperate with each other and share tasks. One of my friends came up with a brilliant idea, a pram pusher for getting babies off to sleep, and put together a design. The other guys did some great creative stuff, making it look really cool and working on the mechanics. My role, although crucial, was a bit less glamorous, designing the electronics to actually make it work. It was a fairly straightforward job, so I wanted to be a bit more creative …

3

Probably the best example is when I used to work as an accounts assistant in a factory. Although my work was mostly administrative, from time to time I had to deal with unpaid invoices, which meant contacting customers and reminding them that they needed to pay. Obviously this was an area that required strong customer service skills. There was one time when one of our regular customers, a guy who ran his own transport company, suddenly stopped paying his invoices, and wouldn't reply to any of my emails. My boss told me to phone and tell him we were going to stop supplying him with goods …

■ 5.2

1

The problem was, it was at exactly the same time as my exam session. I had to choose between studying for my exams and getting involved in the case. Well, I spoke to my professor at university to explain the situation, but he told me it would be impossible to rearrange the exams. Obviously there was no way I'd expect the takeover to wait for a better time for me. I considered trying to do both, and perhaps doing less revision than I needed, but my exams were too important for me to take any risks. In the end I had to put my studies first. When I explained this to my employer, they were actually very supportive, and when they saw how disappointed I was at missing the opportunity, they made sure I got more involved in the next big case that came up. That happened a few months later, and it was a fantastic experience. And because I'd had a chance to study properly, I passed my exams with a very good grade. So it all worked out in the end.

2

My role, although crucial, was a bit less glamorous, designing the electronics to actually make it work. It was a fairly straightforward job, so I wanted to be a bit more creative. Anyway, I put together the electronics very quickly, but I wanted to try something new, so I started playing around with extra features – a remote control, a timer, different speed settings, that sort of thing. I'd never done anything like that before, but it was a great way to learn. The other guys in the team really liked my ideas, so they adapted their designs slightly to take advantage of my modifications. In the end we won the competition, and the judges specifically mentioned my extra features as an important factor in our success. And, of course, I learnt a lot of new skills in the process.

3

My boss told me to phone and tell him we were going to stop supplying him with goods, and to threaten legal action. I wanted to be a bit more delicate because I'd built up quite a good relationship with the customer over the time I'd worked there. So I called him to find out if everything was okay. It turned out his accountant had been taken ill and he was trying to do everything himself, and had got into a mess. Some of his other suppliers were threatening him

with legal action, and he just couldn't deal with all those problems and keep his business going at the same time. I agreed to give him another month to repay, and we continued supplying him during that time. This gave him the freedom to hire a temporary accountant, and within a few days he'd managed to sort everything out. So we actually ended up getting paid within a week, and from then on he was a perfect customer, and recommended us to plenty of other new customers.

■ 5.3

Grace: So, Oliver, what is a competency-based question, and how are they different from traditional interview questions?

Oliver: Well, basically in a traditional interview, the interviewer will ask you questions focused on whether you have the skills and knowledge needed to do the job. Whereas competency-based interview questions go much further, asking you additional questions about your character and personal attributes, to see if you'll fit in to the culture of the company you've applied for work with.

Grace: So basically, behavioural competencies are the character traits and behaviour qualities of an individual, such as the ability to communicate effectively, leadership skills and so on?

Oliver: Exactly. Now in the past it might have been enough to state that you were a team leader on your CV, but employers have quickly realised that this doesn't guarantee that you have good leadership skills. Now you've got to prove these skills in an interview, and interviewers have developed competency-based questions in order to find out if you have these attributes. In these questions the interviewer will be looking for evidence of how you acted in real situations in the past that demonstrate these competencies.

Grace: But wouldn't a candidate have stated these competencies in their CV?

Oliver: Perhaps briefly, but not in any real detail as there's not enough space on a CV to go into any real depth about a specific situation and how you dealt with it. That's what an interview is all about. Interviewers will certainly take your CV and cover letter as a starting point, but then they'll go into much more depth, trying to assess whether you're the right person for the job and the company.

Grace: Is it possible to prepare for a competency-based question?

Oliver: Definitely, and it's essential that you do. Competency-based questions are looking for stories of your actions in the past, and it's these stories that provide evidence of your skills and competencies. It's all about proving you have the right skills and personality for the position.

Grace: So you're saying that candidates should prepare stories that demonstrate evidence of the competencies needed for a particular job?

Oliver: Yes. And it's essential that candidates identify what competencies are needed for a job, and prepare these stories before the interview, otherwise it's likely that their mind will go blank in the middle of the interview and they will be stuck with nothing to say. Or worse, they will simply repeat word-for-word what is written on their CV, which the interviewer has already read.

Grace: Are competency-based questions common in interviews these days?

Oliver: Definitely. Certainly in western-based cultures, they have become almost standard practice in all interviews.

■ 5.4

Neil: Hello, Vicky. My name is Neil Forrest, and this is my colleague Julia Smith. First of all, we'd like to thank you very much for coming here today. We've read your CV and cover letter but wonder if you could tell us a little bit more about your educational background?

Vicky: Yes, of course. I grew up and went to school in Hong Kong. After that I went to City University in Hong Kong where I completed a bachelor's degree in Business Administration. After that I moved to Manchester, where I completed a Master's in Public Relations at Manchester Metropolitan University.

■ 5.5

Neil: Could you tell us something about your educational background?

Pieter: Yes, of course. I did my first degree at the University of Rotterdam. That was a fantastic experience because it was my first time living away from my parents, so it really taught me how to be independent, and of course how to manage conflicting priorities and deadlines. I managed to combine good academic results with active membership of several sports teams. I represented my university in a national rowing competition, which was a wonderful experience. Then when I was in the second year, I was offered the opportunity to take part in an exchange programme at the University of St Petersburg. My university was trying to build up a good relationship with partners in Russia, and they were desperate for volunteers. I thought it would be a once-in-a-lifetime opportunity, so I volunteered. I ended up having a fantastic year there, and made friends with people from all over the world. When I came back, I had a student placement in my third year, when I spent three months doing some market research at a bank. They were trying to find ways of improving customer service, so I helped set up a focus group and analyse the results. Then after my first degree, I moved to America to complete a Psychology Major at Yale.

■ 5.6

Neil: As you know, the position here at Clyde & Johnson's requires somebody with strong communication and organisational skills. Could you tell us about a time when you had to use these skills at work?

Vicky: Yes, of course. At the moment I spend a lot of time travelling between Asia and Europe working with regional teams organising educational events, so I use both of these skills on a regular basis. Let me give you an example. As you know, the Chinese market is growing in all areas, including pharmaceuticals. However, at the time, Green Pharmaceuticals felt they didn't have enough contacts in China. It was clear that the situation wasn't very good for us. We needed to improve things. So in order to increase our number of contacts in China I decided to organise a pharmaceutical conference in Beijing. It was my responsibility to ensure that all the right people were invited. I really had to use all my skills at communicating, in both English and Mandarin, to persuade people to participate. In the end my hard work resulted in a successful conference, with our employees meeting and talking to the right people. As a matter of fact this conference was such a success that it is now an annual event, and has led directly to closer professional relationships between Green Pharmaceuticals and key contacts in China.

5.7

Neil: Tell me about a time when you had to resolve a difficult situation.

Vicky: Okay. There was a time when I was organising a conference here in London. It was a couple of months ago, and it was a really important conference. Anyway, what happened was one of the main guest speakers, who was due to give the opening address, had his flight cancelled and wasn't sure if he was going to make it on time. It was very important the participants were happy with the conference, and I knew they would be disappointed if he didn't show up. So I decided to try and find another flight for the speaker. After a bit of negotiating with a different airline, I managed to get him booked onto a slightly later flight. Unfortunately this meant that even if he came straight from the airport, he would still be a bit late for the opening address. I took a risk and hoped that he wasn't going to be delayed any more. As soon as he'd landed I contacted him, and when I knew he was in a taxi and on his way, which was about five minutes before he was supposed to be on stage, I got up on the stage. I then told the participants about the situation and I invited them to have some coffee and cakes while we waited, which I'd organised beforehand. Actually, they liked this, as it was a chance to network a little and get to know some of the other conference participants. When the speaker did finally arrive, it was actually difficult to get everybody back in the main hall. In the end I managed to keep everybody happy and ensure that the conference went as smoothly as possible.

5.8

Jarek: Hi, Olivia. It's great to see you. How are you?

Olivia: I'm fine. Lots of work, as usual, but I'm really enjoying it at the moment. Anyway, I've got a couple of weeks off coming up, which I'm looking forward to. So, I've heard you've got an interview here on Friday. That's great. I knew you'd get short-listed.

Jarek: I know, it's great, but now I'm a bit stressed about the interview! I was wondering if you could give me an idea about the sorts of questions they might ask me.

Olivia: Sure. My last interview was a while ago now, but I think I can remember what it was like. And I can even tell you what it's like from the other side as I interview people myself now! Do you know who's interviewing you?

Jarek: No, but it was a woman called Sabine Griffin who sent me the email, inviting me in.

Olivia: Oh! If it's Sabine, you'll be fine – she's really nice, super organised. Although you're likely to be interviewed by two or possibly three people, not just her.

Jarek: I thought so. So any tips on what they'll be looking for?

Olivia: Well, first of all, they are going to want to know why you left your last job, what was wrong with it.

Jarek: I hated my last job, I couldn't stand the boss. He used to drive me crazy!

Olivia: I know, but obviously you shouldn't say anything negative about him or your last job. You've got to be positive and think of another good reason for leaving. You should try not to mention any weaknesses or negatives at all during the whole interview. You did quit, didn't you?

Jarek: Yes, I handed in my notice and left as soon as I could. So what do you think I should say?

Olivia: Personally I'd say something like, 'Although I really liked my job, and the people I was working with, I didn't feel I was being stretched enough. I'm looking for a position in which I can develop my professional skills further.' Sounds impressive, doesn't it?

Jarek: Yes, I like it, and it's partly true, but it wasn't the main reason I left.

Olivia: I know, but you've got to play the game. Of course you shouldn't lie about your background, qualifications and experience, but you've got to focus on the positives in every question and avoid any negatives. You should never say anything negative about yourself in the interview.

5.9

1

Well, in the past I sometimes used to procrastinate a little. There were times when I used to put things off until the last minute, when completing an essay for university for example. But I realised that perhaps this wasn't the most effective way of working and so I started setting a strict schedule for all my projects well in advance and set myself personal deadlines. Using a schedule has really helped me and I'm much better organised now and able to take on more projects at the same time.

2

Hmm. My weaknesses? Let me think. Well, in answer to your question you mentioned that the staff here use Apple Macintosh computers. I am not very familiar with Apple Macs and I'm used to using Windows. However, I managed to learn how to use a number of programs very quickly on my own and I'm sure I'd get used to using Apple Macs very quickly. I really enjoy using computers and new gadgets, and I'm always keen to learn how to use new technology.

3

Weaknesses? Well, I can be a bit of a workaholic and always get very involved in every project that I work on. I'm happy to spend a lot of time and energy making sure that every project is as successful as possible. So, occasionally, when I feel that other members of the team might not be working as hard, I can get a little frustrated. I'm aware of this problem, and I try to solve situations like this by being extremely positive and enthusiastic.

5.10

1

I occasionally have a little difficulty making decisions. This is because I pay a lot of attention to detail and make sure that every single decision I make is the best decision possible. Basically, I'm somebody who carefully considers all of the available options before making a choice.

2

I used to be a bit too stubborn and it was sometimes hard to get me to change my mind. A former colleague of mine told me that I was becoming difficult to work with. Well, ever since then I have put significant effort into my team-working skills and now I actively ask for advice and suggestions from my colleagues when making decisions. Last year I was even asked to chair weekly staff meetings while our boss was away on business.

3

When working on projects I am a 'big picture' person. This means that from time to time I might miss some minor details. I've been aware of this for some time. So now when I'm managing a project I make sure that I have the support I need to keep an eye on specific minor details, leaving me free to concentrate on managing the entire project. I think successful management is about getting the right team together and then completely trusting them to do the job you've given them.

5.11

Interviewer: Well, your job sounds very interesting. Considering the fact that you are now seeking employment with us, what is it about your job that you dislike?

Adam: I enjoy a great deal about my current job and have gained a lot of valuable experience in the last three years. However, I'm looking for an opportunity to contribute these skills to a larger organisation such as yours. I'm seeking fresh challenges and the possibility to develop further professionally.

5.12

John: Hello. Can I speak to Alex Mencken please?

Alex: This is Alex. How can I help you?

John: Hello, Alex. My name is John Bradshaw and I'm calling from King's Theatre regarding your recent application for a position with us. Is this a good time for you?

Alex: Oh, I'm very happy you called. Unfortunately I have about ten minutes before I have to leave. Is that enough time, or can you call back later this afternoon?

John: That would be fine. What time is good for you? I'm free after 2pm.

Alex: How about 2.30?

John: Perfect. I'll call you at 2.30.

Alex: Great. I look forward to it.

John: Yes. So do I. Speak to you later. Goodbye.

Alex: Bye.

5.13

John: A large part of the job is managing the logistics of the theatre performances.

Alex: I'm sorry, could you say that again? I didn't quite catch what you said.

John: Yes. Of course. A large part of the job is managing the logistics of the theatre performances.

Alex: Could you tell me what that would involve?

John: Well, basically, it means that the artistic administrator's got to work with everybody at the theatre, from the performers themselves right down to front-of-house staff, security, technical people, stage management, and so on, to ensure that the performances run as smoothly as possible. Oh, and they've got to manage the performance contracts.

Alex: Do you mean booking the singers, musicians, set designers, directors and so on?

John: That's right. You'd also participate in advisory panel meetings a couple of times a year. It sounds like a big job, doesn't it? And it is very important, but there'd be support from the rest of the team.

Alex: I'm having trouble hearing you. Can you hear me clearly?

John: Yes. You're fine on my end. Can you hear me now?

Alex: Oh wait. Okay, that's much better. I'm on my mobile and the reception's not great around here. I live in a black spot! You were talking about what the job would involve.

John: Ah, yes. Well, another part of the job is to participate in advisory panel meetings about four times a year.

Alex: Could you explain what you mean by advisory panel meetings?

John: Yes, of course. It's quite simple really, and one of the most interesting parts of the job. As you know, here at King's Theatre we are trying to support new talent. Part of this means that every couple of months we commission a couple of plays from new writers, which we agree to finance and help develop, until they are ready to put on a showcase performance. We then let them showcase their performances here at the theatre. At the advisory panel meeting we discuss potential projects, and try to select the productions we think have the greatest potential.

 5.14

1
Candidate: Could you explain what you mean by piece rates?

Interviewer: Piecework is a form of performance-related pay, where you would be paid a fixed piece rate for each unit you produce.

2
Candidate: I'm sorry, could you say that again, as I didn't quite catch what you said?

Interviewer: Yes, of course. My name is Mr Johnson and I'm calling to discuss your application for an internship here at Ariel Publishers.

3
Candidate: Do you mean that when the company is busy I would be required to work overtime?

Interviewer: Yes. But of course overtime rates are higher than normal pay.

4
Candidate: I'm having trouble hearing you. Can you hear me clearly?

Interviewer: Yes, I can hear you perfectly this end, although if you can't hear me well, perhaps I'll try and call you back on a landline.

5
Candidate: Your advertisement mentions administrative work. Could you tell me what that would involve?

Interviewer: Well, basically it means keeping our records up-to-date and sending a weekly email to our clients.

6
Candidate: So, if I understand you correctly, what you're saying is the job may involve some overtime?

Interviewer: Yes, but you would be paid extra for this.

6.1

Sophie: Hey, Silvia. So how did it go yesterday?

Silvia: Well, I think it went well. They were really nice and professional. I really hope they'll offer me the job. I'd love to work there.

Sophie: So, did you write and thank them for the interview?

Silvia: What? No. They're going to let me know once they've interviewed the other candidates and made a decision.

Sophie: I know. But you should send them an email or a note thanking them for the interview. It'll make you stand out from the crowd and seem really professional.

Silvia: It sounds good but I don't want to sound desperate, as if I'm begging for the job.

Sophie: Of course not. You're not going to go over the top, just a brief note, telling them that you appreciate their time and that you're serious about the job. I think they'll be impressed more than anything. I would be.

Silvia: I can see your point. Okay, so what do you think I should include in the letter?

6.2

Sophie: Okay. Well, first things first. It's important that you send the note today. Ideally you should send it on the day of the interview.

Silvia: To show I'm professional, right?

Sophie: Exactly. This will impress the interviewer, as most applicants do not do this, showing them that you're organised and professional, as well as keeping you fresh in their mind.

Silvia: Okay. I'll email them today. But what am I going to say?

Sophie: Start by thanking them for having the opportunity of attending an interview. If you can remember some specific things that the interviewer mentioned, it would be good to mention these in the letter. This will show that you recognise the importance of what the interviewer said. All employers are looking for applicants who demonstrate good listening skills and the ability to put received information into practice.

Silvia: So basically, I should show them that I really listened to what they had to say about the job during the interview? And tell them that I want the job?

Sophie: Yes, but try to prove that you really understand what the job will actually involve. Demonstrate that you clearly understand the requirements of the job and the challenges that the job will bring. Identifying these in your letter will then allow you to go on to state confidently how you will be able to do the job, and meet these challenges.

Silvia: I really think I could do the job. I've already got some ideas for some things that I could do if I was given the post.

Sophie: That's great, and exactly the type of thing you should include in your letter. It will help the interviewer to clearly see you doing the job. Concrete practical suggestions for the job will impress the interviewer and put you in a strong position.

Silvia: Their website is really good, but I've got an idea of how I could improve it even further.

Sophie: Excellent. But don't tell them exactly what your idea is. If you just tell them you've got an idea, then this will get them really interested in you and make them want to speak to you again. Although you've got to be sure that your idea is a winner ...

Silvia: It is!

Sophie: Oh, and if you remember something important that you forgot to mention during the interview, then this is the time and place to talk about it. It might be the crucial deciding factor in getting you the job.

Silvia: Thanks, Sophie. As always you've been an enormous help.

Sophie: Well, let me know how you get on and then when they offer you the job we can go out and celebrate!

6.3

Carmen: Hi, Paul. What's up?

Paul: I'm a bit disappointed, actually. I didn't get that job in the bank.

Carmen: Oh no, that's a real shame. You really wanted it, didn't you?

Paul: Yeah. It's so disappointing. And if I wasn't good enough to work in this bank, perhaps I'm not good enough to work in any bank.

Carmen: But it's not that you're not good enough. You got an interview, didn't you? So they must have thought you were good enough to give you an interview.

Paul: But I didn't get the job, did I? How do you explain that?

Carmen: Well, they had to choose somebody, and they must have had lots of strong candidates at the interview. There must have been someone there with even better experience than you, or who performed better on the day in the interview. Or perhaps they already knew who was going to get the job before they started.

Paul: So why go to the bother of arranging interviews?

Carmen: Sometimes companies do that. They have interviews because they have procedures from head office saying they have to do it this way, but the interviewers already have a strong favourite before they start.

Paul: Like the boss's son ...

Carmen: Not necessarily, no. It could be someone who did a student placement there and got on well with everybody. Or someone recommended by someone they know. It could be someone they worked with in a previous company.

Paul: But that's not fair.

Carmen: No, but the world's not always fair. You know what they say, it's not what you know, it's who you know.

Paul: So, I haven't got a chance if they just give jobs to their friends!

Carmen: I'm not saying that's what happens all the time, or even very often. In the majority of cases I'm sure the contest is genuinely open. All I'm saying is that the fact that you were rejected doesn't necessarily mean there's something wrong with you.

Paul: Maybe, but it doesn't make me feel much better.

Carmen: What did they say in the rejection letter?

Paul: Oh, the usual stuff. 'Thank you for coming to the interview, blah blah blah, we regret to inform you that your application has been unsuccessful. If you would like any feedback on your performance, blah blah blah ...'

Carmen: Hang on, that's really good. It means they can tell you what you did wrong, or what you can improve, or why they gave the job to someone else. You've got to request feedback.

Paul: No, I don't feel like it. I'm depressed enough already. I don't need someone listing all the things that are wrong with me.

Carmen: Oh, come on. It's not that bad. They're just normal people after all, and I'm sure they'll be nice and professional. They want to leave you with a good impression. You're still a potential customer, don't forget, and even a potential employee.

Paul: How do you work that out? They rejected me.

Carmen: For this job, yes, but now they know who you are and what you can do, they might consider you for other jobs that are more suitable for your talents. You could be the new 'boss's son', the favourite candidate for the next job.

Paul: Do you really think so?

Carmen: I have no idea. But if you don't ask for feedback, you'll never know.

Paul: Okay, I'll give it a go. How should I do it?

▇▇ 6.4

Alex: Hello. Alex speaking.

John: Hello, Alex. It's John Bradshaw from King's Theatre. I'm delighted to tell you that after careful consideration we would like to offer you the position of administrative assistant.

Alex: Thank you very much. That's very good news.

John: As we discussed during the interview, we are happy to offer you a starting salary of £20,000.

Alex: That's great. I'd like to take some time to consider your offer. Is it okay if I contact you with a decision by tomorrow at the latest?

John: Yes. That's absolutely fine. And if you have any questions in the meantime, please feel free to give me a call.

▇▇ 6.5

Alex: Hey Ella, guess what? King's Theatre called me this morning and offered me the job.

Ella: That's great. You always wanted a job at a theatre in London.

Alex: I know. Even though I know it's going to be expensive, living in a big city, I'm looking forward to moving. It's going to be great.

Ella: So you're sure that this is the right job for you and you're not just accepting the first offer you get? You applied to a couple of theatres, didn't you?

Alex: Yes, I applied to a number of theatres. But I really got on with the interviewer at King's, and the other members of staff that I met were really nice. I could see myself working there. Plus the money's pretty good as well.

Ella: Did you negotiate?

Alex: Well, sort of. They offered me the same starting salary I mentioned during the interview.

Ella: Doesn't that worry you? Perhaps you could have got more if you'd pushed for it?

Alex: Perhaps, but I'm happy with it for now, and if I do well then I'll be in a position to negotiate a raise.

Ella: What about the benefits? How much holiday will you have?

Alex: I'm not really sure, to be honest. We never discussed it.

Ella: If I were you, I'd get that clarified before you officially start work, as you don't want a nasty surprise later on. And what about your course that you've enrolled on? Are you still going to be able to do it?

Alex: Well, I mentioned the course during the interview, and I made it clear that the skills I would gain on the course would help me to do the job much more effectively, so I'm pretty sure they'll let me do it.

Ella: And will they pay you while you do the course?

Alex: I'm not sure.

Ella: Well, I think it's worth contacting them and finding out whether they'll be willing to pay you while you do the course. It's not likely, but it's worth trying.

Alex: You're right. I'll give them a call.

Ella: And then afterwards you should send a formal acceptance letter as well.

Alex: Is that really necessary?

Ella: Well, if you state in writing your understanding of the terms of employment, this will help clear up any potential misunderstandings before they can become a problem.

Alex: So what would I put in it?

Ella: Okay. Get me a pen and a piece of paper and I'll help you plan it.

▇▇ 6.6

Ella: Okay, so in an acceptance letter the first thing to do is thank whoever made you the job offer, and then make it clear that you have decided to accept it.

Alex: Okay, got that. That's it, isn't it?

Ella: Oh no. You're missing the point of writing the letter. You should use your acceptance letter to restate the basic terms of employment as you understood them, including hours per week, salary and benefits.

Alex: And this is the second part of the letter?

Ella: Yes. This letter is not a contract, but putting in writing your understanding of the terms of employment will help avoid any potential misunderstandings.

Alex: I see. What's next?

Ella: Well, then I'd repeat any instructions you were given during the interview, such as your starting date, working hours and so on.

Alex: What about my question about my holiday allowance?

Ella: Yes, this is the time to request clarification of any terms of employment that were vague in the interview or that concerned you afterwards, so your question about holiday leave, for example.

Alex: And that's it?

Ella: Not quite. You've got to end with some more positives, so it's best to express how much you're looking forward to starting the job. You could even mention a couple of aspects of the post that you think you'll particularly enjoy. And of course, you've got to ensure your acceptance letter is professional looking – check it carefully for any grammatical mistakes, typing errors and misspelt words. Actually, on second thoughts why don't you send it to me first and I'll proof read it for you? I know what your emails are like!

▇▇ 6.7

Alex: Hello. This is Alex Mencken. Could you put me through to Karl Osborne please?

Receptionist: Yes, of course. I'll just put you on hold for a minute, and put you through.

Karl: Hello, Alex. What can I do for you? I'm afraid we haven't made a decision yet as we're still in the process of interviewing candidates for the position.

Alex: Yes, I know. Actually, I'm calling as I've been offered a job elsewhere, which I have accepted.

Karl: I see.

Alex: I just wanted to let you know. I also wanted to say that I really enjoyed meeting you. I was very impressed by your team and the working environment at the Cromwell.

Karl: Thank you for saying so. I would say that we were also impressed by your interview and I'm sorry to hear that you've accepted another job. But I understand your decision. I wish you the very best of luck.

Alex: Thank you very much.

Karl: And if things don't work out, make sure that you give me a ring and I'll see if we've got anything we can offer you.

Alex: That's very kind of you. I will do.

Karl: Thanks for letting us know like this.

Alex: It's the least I could do. Thank you for giving me the chance to talk about possible work at the theatre.

▇▇ 6.8

Receptionist: Future Designs, Charlotte speaking.

Tomasz: Hello. My name is Tomasz Filipek. I had an interview with your company last week, for the graphic designer's job. I was wondering if I could speak to Ms Johnson?

Receptionist: Yes, of course. I'll just put you through.

Ms Johnson: Hello, Tomasz. It's good to hear from you.

Tomasz: Hello, Ms Johnson. Thank you very much for offering me the job of graphic designer.

Ms Johnson: You're very welcome. Have you made a decision yet?

Tomasz: Well, I really appreciate the time you spent talking to me about the job and the company and it's been a very difficult decision. However, I have decided not to accept the job.

Ms Johnson: Oh, that's a great shame. Can I ask why?

Tomasz: Well, I was really impressed by the work your company does, especially your advertising campaigns for major retailers, and know it would've been a good opportunity for me. But I've recently been offered another job which I feel is more suited to my skills and interests.

Ms Johnson: I appreciate the fact that you've called to let me know, although it's a shame you won't be joining us. I wish you the best of luck for the future.

Tomasz: Thank you very much and thank you again for your time.

Ms Johnson: You're welcome. Goodbye.

Tomasz: Goodbye.

▇▇ 6.9

1

Employer: What sort of salary are you looking for, Andy?

Andy: Well, in my last job I was paid £18,000 and I'd be hoping to earn more than that now considering my level of experience.

Employer: We would certainly be able to match that, and even offer you slightly more. How does a starting salary of £20,000 sound?

Andy: It sounds very good.

Employer: Excellent. All we need to do now is draw up a contract.

Andy: Great.

2

Employer: What sort of salary are you looking for, Nick?

Nick: Well, I know you are a well-established company with a reputation for looking after your people well, so I expect you will be offering employment at the market rate.

Employer: Yes, that's very true, but we have to start somewhere, so tell me, what are you expecting?

Nick: Perhaps you could tell me what the range is for this position, as I might be tempted to overprice myself if I give a figure.

Employer: Well, the range for this post is between $42,000 and $44,000.

Nick: I see. Given that I have five years' full-time experience in this field, and have an MA, how far up the range would you be able to offer someone like myself?

Employer: We were thinking in the region of $43,000.

Nick: … mmm …

Employer: But in your case, considering your specific previous employment experience we could offer $43,000 plus a $2,000 starting bonus.

Nick: Thank you. Could you tell me how often pay is reviewed here?

Employer: Normally once a year. The next pay review is due in October.

Nick: Would I be entitled to a pay review at this point – subject, of course, to my satisfactory performance in the position?

Employer: Yes, that's reasonable.

■ 6.10

Grace: So, Oliver, what did you think of Andy's salary negotiation? He got what he was looking for.

Oliver: That's true, but I think he was a bit lucky. I very much doubt it would be that easy for most people. Anyway, he doesn't even know what he could have got. He might have got more if he'd played the negotiation game a little better.

Grace: What do you mean?

Oliver: He made the classic mistake of mentioning his desired salary first before establishing what the employer's range for the position was. He may be happy with the offer, but he's unaware that perhaps he could have been offered a higher starting salary. He also failed to discuss any fringe benefits.

Grace: Fringe benefits? You mean things like holiday entitlement, health cover, mobile phone, company car?

Oliver: Exactly. When these are added on to a salary it can make a significant difference.

Grace: I guess you think Nick's approach was much more successful?

Oliver: Yes. His approach was to keep throwing the question back to the employer, forcing him to state a range for the position. It is a proven fact that in almost all negotiation cases, whoever mentions a figure first ends up with the worse deal.

Grace: Yes, that makes a lot of sense, now you mention it. I also really liked the way that after the initial offer was made, Nick stayed silent, which put pressure on the interviewer to improve the first offer.

Oliver: Yes. It worked, but he was also lucky here, as often the interviewer might not have the power to make that decision.

Grace: Yeah, there's no point trying to negotiate if you're not talking to the person who makes the decisions. Another thing I liked about Nick's tactics was that before agreeing to the offer he established when his pay will be reviewed. This opens the door to future increases.

Oliver: Yes, indeed. He agreed to the offer at this point. But do you think he could have got even more?

Grace: If he was extremely confident of his position, and the employer's desire to employ him, he could have continued the negotiation by saying something like, 'I am very keen to join your company. However, I was expecting a larger salary', although that's a pretty risky strategy.

You've got to remember that once you have agreed to an offer, you won't be able to attempt to improve it.

Oliver: Yeah. You've really got to be sure they want you badly to try that. Have you got any other negotiation tips?

Grace: The main piece of advice I'd give is to go into the negotiation knowing the market rate for the job, and the range the employer has for the position. You've got to do your research into the company and know what you've got to offer.

Oliver: Although I would say that when a salary range is given in a job advert, unless you can prove to the interviewer that you have extensive knowledge of the job and the organisation, you would probably be offered the post at the lower end of the scale.

Grace: That's true, but as long as you're negotiating from a position of power, when you know they really want you, and you're talking to the decision makers, you've got a real chance.

Oliver: Yes, you certainly can't negotiate when you're still one of many candidates, even if you have been short-listed. Only once you are the final candidate, the one they want to hire, should you start any negotiations.

ANSWER KEY

Student A's role play cards for Exercise 7g on page 83:

Student A: Employer	Possible score	Actual score
Salary:		
Salary €27,500 pa	250	
For every €500 more	–30	
For every €500 less	50	
Holiday:		
20 days' holiday	50	
For every day more	–20	
For every day less	30	
Benefits:		
Company car	–50	
Mobile phone	–5	
Pay review in six months	–30	
Total points:		

Student A: Candidate	Possible score	Actual score
Salary:		
Salary €22,000 pa	200	
For every €500 more	50	
For every €500 less	–50	
Holiday:		
28 days' holiday	100	
For every day more	20	
For every day less	–50	
Benefits:		
Company car	50	
Mobile phone	10	
Pay review in six months	10	
Total points:		

Unit 1

1a
1 c   2 g   3 d   4 f   5 b   6 a
7 h   8 e

b
Suggested answer
8 7 6 1/2 5 4 3

c
1 g (*Customer service assistant, Packaging Palace*)
2 c (*recent psychology graduate*); g (*BSc (Hons) Psychology (2.1)*); h (*recent psychology graduate*)
3 a (*circa £25k pa*)
4 e (*a bit moody / not very well-organised / make decisions without thinking*); f (*I didn't use to be very well-organised*)
5 d (*and calculated … you could justify charges of …*); e (*good at maths*); g (*Liaised with management on pricing strategy*)
6 c (*as advertised in* The Guardian); h (*an advert in* The Guardian)
7 e (*doing research on the net*)
8 a (*an ability to work well in a team*); d (*make a very useful contribution to your team*); e (*work well with people*)
9 b (*It all looks very impressive*); c (*a successful international firm*); d (*Everyone in your office was friendly and made me feel very welcome … your strong reputation for quality*); h (*your excellent reputation*)
10 d (*I checked your prices*)

d
Teresa meets the advertised criteria: she has a degree and related professional experience in sales and marketing. The extract from her letter demonstrates a clear, confident and professional approach, which helped her get an interview. Her chances of getting the job appear strong, but this will depend on her ability to emphasise her teamworking skills and play down her weak organisational skills during her interview.

2a
1 Sophie suggests Silvia works out what she wants to do by thinking about what she likes doing and what she's interested in.
2 She thinks about something she's done that was successful, and then tries to identify the skills she used.
3 No, she says that Silvia shouldn't take them too seriously.
4 A successful job search is not just about finding a job that you would be good at, but about finding a job that you will love doing.

3a
b to   c at   d to   e in   f in   g in
h at   i to   j at

b
2 Achievements
3 Languages
4 Experience
5 Personal characteristics
6 Knowledge

c
1 To start looking for a new job
2 Because his company is too small to give him the experience he wants
3 Coming up with new ideas and suggesting alternative solutions
4 To speak Mandarin
5 He is taking Mandarin lessons and listening to podcasts.

d
flexible: *I'm very adaptable. I don't mind working late or at weekends, and I'll have a go at anything …*
creative: *I'm also good at coming up with new ideas and suggesting alternative solutions; you used to stick notes with new ideas everywhere*
disorganised: *Your desk was such a mess and you never knew where anything was.*

e
2 c   3 e   4 d   5 b   6 a

f
2 indecisive
3 inflexible
4 disorganised
5 unpersuasive
6 unreliable

4a
2 read; completed (obtained)
3 graduated; hold; completed (obtained)
4 graduating; awarded; read

b
1 from; with; in
2 in; with; from
3 in; from; in
4 at

5b
2 d   3 a   4 g   5 e   6 h   7 c   8 b

c
Suggested answers
1 flexibility: I am willing to investigate options in depth, even when they are the ideas of others. I am able to adapt to and work with a variety of situations, individuals and groups. I am able to think on my feet. I am willing to try different approaches.
2 leadership skills: I am good at leading, encouraging, inspiring and supporting others to develop confidence and help them to realise their full potential. I delegate routine elements of more complex tasks at work and encourage others to do the same. I am approachable at work.
3 organisational skills: I am always on time at work, attending meetings, and when I cannot make it, I always let somebody know in advance. I can plan ahead and am excellent at meeting deadlines.
4 teamworking skills: I cooperate to meet shared goals even at the expense of my own personal preferences. I listen carefully to the concerns and opinions of others. I enjoy collaborating on projects.

e
1 When she was working in Africa
2 She worked for an NGO (non-governmental organisation) as part of a large team of people, educating local people about the importance of reforestation.
3 She was the communications officer of the student union.

f
1 planning
2 worked; given
3 talked; convinced
4 dealing; understood

g
1 organisational skills
2 flexibility / teamworking skills
3 negotiation/communication skills
4 communication/organisational skills

h
1 b analyse c conduct
2 a invent b suggest c solve
3 a write b explain c give
4 a resolve b listen c work
5 a chair b motivate c delegate
6 a meet b decide c implement
7 a discuss b contribute c support
8 a change b negotiate c convince

6b
1 the Internet
2 networking
3 job agencies / headhunters
4 newspapers and magazines
5 cold calling / mailing

7b
Eryk's technique is more successful.

c
1 b 2 a 3 e 4 d 5 c

d
b 5 c 3; 4 d 2; 4 e 1

8a
Suggested answers
1 The main details of the job; clear instructions for responding; the deadline for submission of applications (often called the closing date); the name and title of the person to whom enquiries can be made if you wish to have a preliminary discussion about the role and your qualifications before submitting the written application; the name, title and address of the person or business unit to whom the response should be sent – this is often a different person from the one who is responsible for the actual job; whether applications are to be submitted electronically or mailed; whether a detailed job description is available; whether there are key selection criteria (the standards or requirements you must meet to be considered for the role); what qualifications, if any, are required; whether a website address is provided for more information about the company
2 An advertisement that gives a sense of what the organisation is like

b
2 curriculum vitae
3 experience
4 agency
5 on-target earnings
6 per annum
7 per week
8 point of sale

c
1 EXP 2 PA 3 AGY 4 POS
5 OTE (if a salesperson hits the targets specified for them, they will be guaranteed that amount of money)

d
Almost all employers want employees who will fit in with the rest of the team (*team player*), will help the company make money (*results-focused*), can think intelligently and come up with new ideas (*dynamic*), can meet deadlines under pressure (*good organisational skills*) and are willing to work longer hours when necessary (*flexible*).

e
1 team player 4 flexible
2 results-focused 5 good organisational skills
3 dynamic

f
1 Media assistant (*We are looking for a … graduate*) The trainee finance recruitment consultant can be a *graduate or of graduate calibre.*
2 Trainee finance recruitment consultant (*no two days are the same*)
3 Trainee finance recruitment consultant (*£30–£35K*)
4 *Email your CV and cover letter to colm@MediaX.com by May 23rd.*
5 You will be contacted by them (*only successful candidates will be contacted*)

g
1 circa (sometimes abbreviated as *c.* or *ca*)
2 Closing date
3 K
4 Quote Ref
5 pro rata

h
1 Trainee finance recruitment consultant: multi-tasker / target driven / articulate / determined / interpersonal skills / negotiation skills
Media assistant: organisational skills / proof-reading / editing / IT skills / communication skills / language skills
2 Trainee finance recruitment consultant

i
proficiency in = very experienced
excellent command of = very good knowledge of
working knowledge of = basic understanding of

k
1 X is necessary; the successful candidate will be; X is vital; you must be; you will have
2 X would be desirable; ideally you will have; X would be a plus; X is preferred; X would be advantageous; X would be welcome

l
Trainee finance recruitment consultant: *You will have*; *You must be*
Media assistant: *essential*; *would be a plus*; *would be advantageous*

m
1 resourceful 4 computer literate
2 fluent 5 numerate
3 adaptable

n
You would need to be an excellent communicator with fluent English language skills, resourceful, adaptable, with good research skills, able to use a computer well, able to deal with numbers, with a relevant degree and experience in or knowledge of sustainability issues.

■■■ Unit 2

1a
1 curriculum vitae
2 resume / résumé
3 The main purpose of a CV is to persuade a potential employer that you have the right skills, experience, education and personality for the job.
4 A successful CV is the product of careful thought and planning. It needs to stand out from potentially hundreds of competing applicants. In order to do this a CV must be planned and written specifically for the job you are applying for, clearly expressing how you meet the requirements for the job. A successful CV must be concise, honest and error-free.

5 There is no limit to the number of sections in a CV, although all CVs should cover professional experience, educational qualifications and skills. The only rule to remember is that the sections within your CV should all be strictly relevant to the position you are applying for.
6 There is no one correct way to structure your CV, although the two most common approaches are the conventional chronological CV and the skills-based CV.

b
1 Conventional chronological CV and skills-based CV
2 A chronological CV lists your academic achievements and work experience in chronological order. A skills-based CV lists your key transferable skills relevant to the job and provides evidence of these skills.

c
2 Contact 3 Personal statement 4 Education
5 Work experience 6 interests 7 skills
8 References 9 Your name 10 Contact details
11 Personal statement 12 skills
13 Work experience 14 Education 15 Interests
16 Referees

d
The first CV on page 20 is a chronological CV.
The second CV on page 21 is a skills-based CV.

e
2 Developed 7 Held
3 Persuaded 8 Researched
4 Represented 9 Achieved
5 Completed 10 Coordinated (Organised)
6 Organised (Coordinated)

f
1 Communication and teamwork
2 Energy and motivation
3 Adaptability and resourcefulness
4 Research and computer skills

g
1 Both career changers and recent graduates may not have much relevant professional experience, so they may prefer to use a skills-based CV, where capability is emphasised over experience.

2a
Suggested answers
Sending the same CV for all the jobs they apply to; making spelling mistakes; including information that is not relevant; providing too much information so that the CV is too long (more than two pages); using a bad layout or design; including lies

c
1 receive; correspondence; liaise; practice / to practise; advice / to advise
2 Employers don't have much time and a concise CV can demonstrate your ability to edit effectively.
3 Your CV is a legal contract and you could lose your job if found out. You'll be more confident in the interview if your CV is accurate.
4 No, you should adapt your CV for each job you apply for.

d
1 ~~prevous~~ previous; ~~responsable~~ responsible; ~~dealling~~ dealing; ~~correspondance~~ correspondence; ~~massages~~ messages; ~~arrangeing~~ arranging; ~~apointments~~ appointments

2 ~~form~~ from; ~~beneffits~~ benefits; ~~experiance~~ experience; ~~off~~ of; ~~studing~~ studying; ~~abraod~~ abroad; ~~practice~~ practise; ~~foriegn~~ foreign; ~~develope~~ develop; ~~strenghts~~ strengths
3 ~~assistent~~ assistant; ~~personal~~ personnel; ~~acheivement~~ achievement; ~~lead~~ led; ~~witch~~ which; ~~improveing~~ improving; ~~startegic~~ strategic; ~~buisness~~ business; ~~planing~~ planning

3a
1 *Geography graduate; Currently completing Master's in Development Studies with specific focus on sustainability.*
2 *Well-organised, highly motivated; Self-motivated, resourceful and able to motivate others, with excellent communication and interpersonal skills.*
3 *communications strategy adviser*
4 *with recent professional experience developing communication strategy for positive change*
5 *Geography graduate with recent professional experience developing communication strategy for positive change.*

b
b *Well-organised, highly motivated communications strategy adviser.*
c *Geography graduate with recent professional experience developing communication strategy for positive change.*
d *Fluent spoken and written English.*
e *Currently completing Master's in Development Studies with specific focus on sustainability.*

c
1 well-organised; confidently and effectively
2 full-time professional; Proven ability; experience in

d
1 The first is shorter and less factual than Silvia's. The language is strong and positive, but is mostly descriptive. The second is similar to Silvia's in length and style. Character descriptions are supported with evidence.
2 The first statement answers questions **a** and **d**, but does not support the character descriptions with evidence. The four sentences of the second statement mainly answer questions **b**, **d**, **d** again and **b** again.

e
With its stronger focus on professional skills and experience, the second statement is more suitable for this post, which requires previous experience.

g
Adjective 1: enthusiastic; professional. Other suggestions: dedicated, innovative, reliable, organised, ambitious, dynamic, flexible
Sort of person: motivator; team leader. Other suggestions: purchasing executive, brand manager, IT specialist, presenter and trainer, team player
Adjective 2: broad; consistently high. Other suggestions: first-class, numerous, wide-ranging, thorough, specialist, high-quality
Experience/skills: ability to; interest in. Other suggestions: background in, understanding of, reputation for, people-management skills

4b
Note that the three categories are intended only to generate ideas; some section titles may belong to more than one category.

Suggested answers
Personal strengths and competencies: these include anything that tells employers what sort of person you are (e.g. *Flexibility, Initiative, Focus on results, Teamworking, Cross-functional working, Organisational skills*)
Areas of professional experience: what sorts of jobs you have done (e.g. *Accounting, Electronic engineering*) and what objective evidence you can provide of your professional achievements (e.g. an architect might list *Professional awards* or *Major buildings designed*)
Business skills: what you have learnt through your work (e.g. *Negotiation skills, Project management, Communication skills*)

5b
2 creativity
3 analysis
4 writing
5 research
6 teamwork

e
Adjectives and adverbs

f
1 successful
2 successfully
3 successful
4 fully; international
5 wide
6 successful; entire
7 top
8 in-depth
9 substantial
10 excellent

6b
1 b   2 a

e
She used: achieved; coordinated; developed; established; improved; led; organised; persuaded; planned; represented; researched
She used these other verbs: completed; held; liaised; managed; maintained; provided; worked

f
Suggested answers
2 Successfully completed a financial management course.
3 Translated the company website into three different languages.
4 Identified a problem with the company's database system and recommended an alternative solution.
5 Designed and implemented a new customer feedback system, leading to a 20% increase in customer satisfaction levels.

g
Suggested answers
2 Represented front-office staff on ICT Strategy Implementation Team.
3 Formulated training plan.
4 Supervised office budget.
5 Researched and evaluated new suppliers.
6 Presented client feedback questionnaire.
7 Investigated waste reduction.
8 Led design team.

h
1 Answering the phone; filling in forms; taking minutes
2 Dealing with customers; representing the company; listening and writing intelligently; producing company documents
3 Nanny; waitress; cleaner
4 They demonstrate her language skills, and that she's responsible, flexible and hard-working.

i
Professional experience
2007– PA to Managing Director (London)
present • Schedule MD's meetings
       • Represent MD and company with official visitors and on telephone
       • Take minutes at board meetings and write professional official company reports
2007   Nanny (New York)
       • Supervised two English-speaking children (aged 4 and 6)
       • Planned and organised inspiring and educational daily activities
2006   Waitress (Madrid)
       • Developed excellent customer-service skills in Spanish
2006   Chambermaid (Madrid)
       • Maintained hotel rooms at five-star levels of professional presentation
       • Demonstrated flexibility and dedication while developing Spanish language skills

7a
See article in unit

b
1 Because their education experience is more relevant
2 *in skeletal form*
3 If they were your highest educational qualification or they were particularly good
4 Most recent first (*in reverse chronological order*)
5 Add an additional relevant section on IT skills

c
1 PhD
2 Master's degree
3 Bachelor's degree
4 A-levels
5 GCSEs

f
1 Because the title of their degree is not clear enough to explain what the course actually involved. Employers need to know what you actually studied, and not just the name of your degree.
3 The writer has included details of a work placement, an exchange year and a major piece of research (dissertation).

h
Geography graduate with recent professional experience of developing communication strategy for positive change.
Currently completing Master's in Development Studies with specific focus on sustainability.
I researched top international universities for my degree course.
I am currently completing in-depth research on reforestation techniques for the African subcontinent for my Master's degree dissertation.
Research for my dissertation includes substantial use of the Internet and professional journals, and interviewing experts in the field.

8a
2 Employers want to know more than just your qualifications and work experience; they want to know what type of person you are, and whether you are going to fit in.

b
1 The V in CV stands for *vitae*, which is Latin for 'life'. This is relevant as the interests section is about your life and personality.
2 Because it didn't give details of his achievements as captain
3 It shows that you can fit into different environments easily.

4   Her ability to learn new languages quickly
    and that she is a member of an orchestra
5   Running the London Marathon and raising
    £1900 for charity

c
1   leadership skills
2   determination; self-motivation
3   intercultural awareness; language skills
4   analytical skills; intelligence
5   creativity; resourcefulness

g
Suggested answers
2   Keen mountain climber: Recently completed
    a five-day expedition in the French Alps.
    Currently attending a mountain leadership
    course.
3   Passionate photographer: Currently
    attending evening classes to develop my
    photography skills. Excellent working
    knowledge of Photoshop software. Designed
    a website to display my best photographs.
4   University Social Coordinator: Active member
    of the student committee. Organised more
    than ten musical and cultural events.
    Responsibilities included booking acts to
    perform and organising the tickets sales.

9a
See advice in Exercise 9b

b
b 5   c 7   d 6   e 3   f 4   g 1

d
1   1 B   2 G   3 O
2   1 Friends can't comment on your
    professional performance. 2 Employers only
    contact referees to confirm the facts on a CV.
    3 It takes up valuable space, and employers
    are unlikely to contact referees at the early
    stages of the process.
3   *References available on request*

■ Unit 3

1a
1   See article in unit

b
2   cover letter   7   well-focused
3   complement   8   interview
4   persuade   9   business
5   position   10   introduction
6   employer

c
letter of application

e
1   Three years
2   She feels her career prospects are limited at
    Green Pharmaceuticals.

f
2   ✔ (*remember not to be too informal as you
    want to sound as professional as possible*)
3   ✗ (*every cover letter should be written
    specifically for the position you're applying
    for*)
4   ✔ (*You should show that you've read about
    the company, done some research*)
5   ✔ (*you should concentrate on demonstrating
    the skills that are required for the post, what
    you can offer the company*)
6   ✗ (*If a company wants to see any documents
    like that, they'll ask for them later.*)

h
1   Economics
2   Costcutter
3   She sings in and manages a jazz band, and is
    learning Italian.

i
2 l   3 c   4 k   5 g   6 f   7 j
8 h   9 b   10 d   11 e   12 i

j
1   Paragraph 2   4   Paragraph 1
2   Paragraph 5   5   Paragraph 4
3   Paragraph 3

2a
1   enquire
2   response; enclosed
3   recommended; requirements
4   advertised; qualified
5   application; consideration

b
1 b   2 a   3 c   4 a   5 a
All of these approaches could potentially lead to
successful employment. However, your chances
of employment are strongest following a personal
recommendation. Replying to an advertisement
is more likely to lead to a job than applying 'cold'.

c
See advice in audioscript 3.3 on page 87

d
Order: 3 2 1

e
Advice given: specifically mention the position
you are applying for and how you found out
about it; don't copy phrases from the company
website – reformulate them into your own words;
focus on the skills and experience you have
that make you the right person for the job; be
confident in your cover letter but don't make
claims that are difficult to support

3a
1   The main body is the longest section. This
    may be a single powerful paragraph or two or
    three shorter paragraphs. Ideally your cover
    letter should be no longer than a single side
    of A4 paper.
2   Recruitment experts suggest identifying three
    to four specific skills and/or experiences you
    have that meet the requirements for the
    position.
3   Every job you apply for will require a different
    cover letter as you need to demonstrate how
    your skills and experience match the specific
    requirements for each position.

b
2   flexibility (*We often have to work
    unsociable hours under difficult conditions*);
    interpersonal skills (*I ensure that team
    morale is maintained by regularly counselling
    team members to check they are coping with
    the demands of the job*)
3   customer service skills (*I learned that
    customer service is the key to success in the
    service industry*); initiative (*I implemented
    a new way for customer feedback to be
    recorded*)
4   customer service skills (*Working in the shop
    helped me to learn the importance of dealing
    with customers in a friendly and efficient
    way*); entrepreneurial skills (*During this
    month I suggested changing the layout of
    some of the gift displays*)
5   leadership skills (*I have a strong history
    of staff management*); self-awareness (*I
    regularly seek feedback on my performance
    from my superiors and colleagues to identify
    areas I need to improve in*)

c
Suggested answers
2   Within my role as ..., I am responsible for
    ...; We often have to work unsociable hours
    under difficult conditions; I ensure that team
    morale is maintained by ...
3   I implemented a new ...; I believe I can
    apply the skills obtained from my previous
    employment to this position
4   Working in ... helped me to learn the
    importance of ...; During ... I suggested ...;
    These changes led to a significant increase
    in ...
5   I have a strong history of ...; I regularly
    seek feedback on my performance from my
    superiors and colleagues to identify areas I
    need to improve in.

4a
1   You will highlight different skills and
    experience in response to the particular
    skills and experience relevant for the position
    applied for.
2   By reading the advertisement carefully and
    using your knowledge and research of the
    company and the position
3   No

b
1   Public Relations Officer
2   Press Officer for the Swedish Ministry of
    Industry
3   Political Science
4   Hanna has gained professional experience
    as a Press Officer for the Swedish Ministry
    of Industry and also at the Swedish Embassy
    in Warsaw. Through these experiences she
    has developed the following skills: teamwork,
    organisational skills, drafting skills, project
    management skills and linguistic skills. She
    has also gained a substantial amount of
    political and diplomatic knowledge, which is
    relevant for her application to the Australian
    Embassy.

c
2 g   3 a   4 d   5 f   6 h
7 e   8 c

d
Skills: organisational skills, report-writing skills,
summarising skills, teamwork, resourcefulness
(ability to work independently), time-
management skills
Experience: public relations and media-related
fields; knowledge of the Swedish government,
economy, business and EU processes

e
2 a/b/h   3 f   4 d/g   5 b/c   6 e

f
Suggested answers
I am writing in response to your advertisement
for the position of ...; I am currently working as
a(n) ... for ...; Previous experience at ... gave
me an opportunity to ...; During my time there I
learnt to ...; I am very suited to ... and feel this
move would be a logical career step; The role of
... would allow me to develop my existing skills

g
2   During my time
3   As part of my; where I gained
4   During my period of employment at; having
5   In the course of my current job; As a result
6   Since I work with

5a
1 T   2 F   3 T   4 T

b

Jane and Hanna both followed the true advice in Exercise 5a.

c

The American approach (1 and 3) is much more direct and assertive than the British approach (2 and 4). When applying for jobs in America, or to an American company, it is common for applicants to promote themselves strongly and practically assume that an interview is guaranteed. In America it is common to follow up your application with a phone call. In Britain the language used is different and less direct. When applying to a British company it would be inappropriate to assume that an interview is automatic, and it's best to finish the letter by thanking the reader for their time and consideration.

d

1   Extracts 2 and 4

e

See advice in audioscript 3.4 on page 87

f

Advice given: use a professional and appropriate tone: formal, friendly and polite; do not make unsupported claims, or claims that will be difficult to support if you are invited to an interview; thank the company for their time and consideration

6a

2	additional	10	tell
3	want	11	employer
4	require	12	more
5	talk about	13	looking
6	contact	14	request
7	about	15	employment
8	ensure	16	show
9	give		

b

2   searching; employment
3   discuss; greater/further
4   provide; with
5   require; further (we do not say ~~greater information~~); regarding; contact

Should is a more formal equivalent of *if*. It is common in cover letters. Like all modal verbs, *should* is followed by infinitive without *to* (*If my application **is** successful = **Should** my application **be** successful*).

c

Suggested answers

2   to enquire whether you currently have any vacancies
3   the position of financial administrator
4   meet the requirements for the advertised position
5   recommended that I contact you regarding
6   I attach
7   Should you require any further information concerning
8   I would like to thank you in advance

d

Suggested answer

I am writing to apply for the position of secretary, which is advertised on your website. I am currently employed as a secretary at Gordon's Financial Services in Barcelona, a position I have held for three years. I am searching for new employment in Italy, as my husband has recently been asked by his company to move to Milan. I understand that Carnali Carretta is one of the leading financial service providers in Italy.
Six years' international experience in the area of financial services has helped me to develop the

knowledge and skills that a market leader such as Carnali Carretta requires.
If you would like to meet to discuss how my skills and experience can benefit your company in the future, I would welcome the opportunity to come in and meet you.
Yours sincerely,
Jane Nuttall

7b

2 c   3 d   4 g   5 h   6 j   7 m   8 l
9 k   10 o   11 n 12 i 13 f   14 e 15 a

▄▄▄ Unit 4

2b

Ways of creating a positive first impression include: arriving on time; dressing appropriately for the interview; smiling; acting in a confident, relaxed way. Demonstrate that you have done some research into the company, know what you are talking about, and speak using clear, concise, positive language.

d

1	do	4	do
2	do	5	do
3	don't	6	don't

She also suggests: taking an umbrella; taking a contact number in case you are delayed; wearing smart, formal clothes; tying back long hair; checking your social networking pages for any potentially 'damaging' content and to ensure that they make you come across as a professional person.

3a

1   He was in a meeting.
2   A company brochure
3   That two other candidates are being interviewed
4   By paying a compliment about the office
5   Transport and the weather
6   By saying that he has heard positive things about the company (*You were highly recommended*)

b

1   It is vitally important to be professional and polite to *everybody* you meet during an interview. The receptionist may also be asked his or her opinion of the candidate.
2   She asks how many applicants are being interviewed for the position. Knowing how many other candidates she is competing against will help Silvia get a better idea of her chances of success.
3   It is usually positive to mention people you know who currently work for the company. Obviously, it is important that you are confident this person will speak highly of you and also that they are respected within the company.

c

2 b   3 h   4 f   5 d   6 a   7 c   8 e

e

2 e; R   3 d; B   4 b; R   5 g; B   6 j; B
7 f; B   8 i; R   9 h; B   10 a; R

4a

1   Slouching or leaning back in the chair; giving the impression that you are too casual about the job; flapping your hands around a lot when you speak; folding your arms, making you appear defensive; staring at the floor or focusing too much on one interviewer in a panel; talking too fast, slow, etc.
2   Sit reasonably upright to create a more positive professional impression; hold your hands together to avoid unnecessary

movements (although moderate hand movements are perfectly acceptable and can enliven the conversation); keep your arms open and resting on your lap; maintain good eye contact with the interviewer who asked you the question, but glance from time to time at the other interviewers (this can also help you judge the interviewer's reaction to what you are saying); try not to talk too fast and keep your tone moderate; take a deep breath before you start to answer a question and try to keep your answers concise

b

2 a; C   3 e; A   4 c; D   5 d; B

5a

1   See Appendix 2 on page 110 for a list of commonly-asked questions

b

2 c   3 c   4 a   5 b   6 b   7 a
8 c   9 a   10 a & c 11 b   12 a

c

Suggested answers

a   What kinds of things do you worry about? Would you say you're an ambitious person?
b   What do you think of our product range? Do you think this is the sort of company you'd like to work for?
c   How much autonomy to make decisions did you have in your last position? How good is your written English?

e

1   Question 12   3   Question 10
2   Question 7

f

Extract 1 would be better if it were more concise, clear and explicit. The candidate also makes negative comments (*being stuck in a boring job*; *I wouldn't want to get stressed*), which should be avoided.
Extract 2 would be better if it was a little more balanced – it is too positive. Also, the candidate makes some very big claims without providing any evidence in support of them.
Extract 3 would be better if it were better structured. At the moment it is badly organised and confusing.

g

2 e   3 d   4 b   5 a
Extract 1: not clear and explicit
Extract 2: not truthful
Extract 3: not concise

h

See audioscript 4.5 on page 89

i

The candidate's improved response is well-structured, concise and positive. She welcomes responsibility (*which will make me proud of the work I do*), and explains how she will avoid stress (*I'll make sure I only take on what I can manage*). She uses *will* instead of *would* throughout her response, which conveys a positive and optimistic attitude.

j

See audioscript 4.6 on page 89

6b

Suggested answers

1   Alejandro could improve his answer by: speaking for longer and providing a fuller response; not simply repeating details from his CV; using the question as an opportunity to demonstrate his skills and experience relevant to the position he is being interviewed for.

2 Alejandro could improve his answer by: providing more detail about what he has learnt, rather than just listing the modules of his course; relating his answer to the requirements of the position; providing concrete examples of transferable skills he developed at university.

3 Alejandro could improve his answer by: keeping his answer brief and well-structured; only mentioning common professional concerns, which have either been addressed or would not affect his ability to do the job.

4 Alejandro could improve his answer by: providing a much fuller response; talking about his career plans which include his prospective employer.

d

1 Alejandro uses this question as an opportunity to demonstrate the skills and experience relevant for the post he is applying for. He demonstrates high levels of motivation and achievement (*I put a lot of effort into everything I do; our team managed to reach the regional final*) as well as organisational and communication skills (*I had to organise matches and motivate the players*).

2 He uses this question to highlight transferable skills relevant for the job which he has obtained through his time at university (*there were many elements of the degree that could be applied to the business world; This helped me to develop my prioritising skills and ability to work to tight deadlines.*)

3 Alejandro admits to worrying about meeting deadlines. However, as long as he can demonstrate that he is able to meet them, then this response is likely to be seen as a strength rather than as a weakness. He also uses this potentially difficult question to highlight how he has overcome a problem.

4 He emphasises his desire to work for the company (*I'm very keen to get a job with a company such as yours*), whilst also reminding the interviewer of the reasons why he is a strong candidate (*my degree and professional experience; I am a dedicated worker*).

e

2	motivate	8	meeting
3	communicate	9	getting
4	leading	10	get
5	applied	11	make
6	develop	12	gain
7	work		

f

Suggested answers

As … it was essential that I was able to do … effectively; This helped me to develop my … skills and ability to do …; I'm very keen to get a job with a company such as yours where I can …

7c

b 2   c 3   d 2   e 1   f 4   g 3   h 4

d

Lidia follows the recruitment consultants' advice and is the stronger candidate.

e

2	research	5	regularly
3	reputation	6	keen
4	recently	7	spent

8a

1 She researched the market and Futerra in depth.

2 The fact that they work with a range of clients in a variety of sectors

3 Her communications skills and experience in developing communication strategies

4 That it was very attractive and professional

5 A small organisation

b

2 look at your website
3 attracted me to
4 well-established reputation
5 dynamic place to work
6 It's clear from
7 from everything I've learnt

d

Suggested answers

Futerra came out on top; *just what I'm looking for*; *This impressed me a lot*; *a well-established reputation*; *very attractive and professional, really excellent*; *an exciting, dynamic place to work*.

More examples of positive language: I really like the way you … / The best thing about your company is … / A really nice combination of … / What struck me was … / wonderful / amazing / professional / perfect / impressive / attractive / progressive / user-friendly

e

2	enjoyable	4	fulfilling
3	first-class	5	fantastic

9a

1 Good customer service skills

2 She was studying at university in Turin.

3 She managed the volleyball team's finances and has professional experience as a sales assistant.

4 Her knowledge of three languages demonstrates that she is multilingual, but this alone does not demonstrate her communication skills.

b

2 dealing with customers
3 fluently
4 managing people
5 captain of the volleyball team
6 highly effective communicator
7 well under pressure
8 delegate effectively

e

Silvia highlights her communication skills, teamworking skills and research skills.

f

2	years ago	9	So
3	ever since	10	For my dissertation
4	Following	11	So to sum up
5	That's really when	12	for three reasons
6	also when	13	Firstly
7	For example	14	Secondly
8	When I was at	15	finally

g

Suggested answers

I understand the issues you deal with (*and am passionate about them*); *I started getting interested in …*; *I started learning about …*; *I was responsible for* (*dealing with*) *…*; *I know you're* (*also*) *looking for someone who's good at …*; *For my … I'm researching …*; *I think I'm suitable for the position at … for three reasons.*

h

Correct order: 4 1 3 5 2

1b

Speaker 1: Q1   Speaker 3: Q2
Speaker 2: Q4

e

1 Employers are looking for evidence that you have the specific competencies required for the position, e.g. communication skills, leadership qualities, flexibility.

2 Brief stories will provide evidence of how you acted in real situations in the past, which will help you demonstrate the competencies the employer is looking for.

3 They are very common.

g

Situation   Target   Action   Result

h

1 S: *The problem was, it was at exactly the same time as my exam session.*
T: *I had to choose between studying for my exams and getting involved in the case.*
A1: *I spoke to my professor at university to explain the situation,*
A2: *In the end I had to put my studies first.*
R1: *When I explained this to my employer, they were actually very supportive, and when they saw how disappointed I was at missing the opportunity, they made sure I got more involved in the next big case that came up.*
R2: *And because I'd had a chance to study properly, I passed my exams with a very good grade.*

2 S: *My role, although crucial, was a bit less glamorous, designing the electronics to actually make it work.*
T: *I wanted to be a bit more creative.*
A: *I started playing around with extra features …*
R1: *The other guys in the team really liked my ideas, so they adapted their designs slightly to take advantage of my modifications.*
R2: *In the end we won the competition, and the judges specifically mentioned my extra features as an important factor in our success. And, of course, I learnt a lot of new skills in the process.*

3 S: *My boss told me to phone and tell him we were going to stop supplying him with goods, and to threaten legal action.*
T: *I wanted to be a bit more delicate because I'd built up quite a good relationship with the customer over the time I'd worked there.*
A1: *So I called him to find out if everything was okay.*
A2: *I agreed to give him another month to repay, and we continued supplying him during that time.*
R: *So we actually ended up getting paid within a week, and from then on he was a perfect customer, and recommended us to plenty of other new customers.*

i

1 worked out
2 turned out
3 ended up

2a

1 Hong Kong
2 City University in Hong Kong and Manchester Metropolitan University

b
1 The University of Rotterdam
2 He spent a year there after volunteering to take part in an exchange programme.
3 At a bank, doing market research

c
Vicky has provided a standard response to this question. It's not a terrible answer but it's a wasted opportunity. She has simply repeated details that are on her CV, which the interviewers clearly stated they had read. During interviews try not to repeat information straight from your CV. Pieter has taken full advantage of the question, telling the interviewer short stories based on the skills and experience he gained during his time at university in The Netherlands and Russia. He has used the question as an opportunity to demonstrate his relevant competencies.

d
Pieter demonstrates or suggests the following competencies: organisational skills (*it really taught me how to be independent, and of course how to manage conflicting priorities and deadlines*); teamworking (*active membership of several sports teams*); interpersonal skills (*made friends with people from all over the world*); customer service skills (*I helped set up a focus group and analyse the results*)

f
1 They didn't have enough contacts in China.
2 She organised a pharmaceutical conference in Beijing.
3 The conference was a success and led to closer professional relationships between Green Pharmaceuticals and key contacts in China.

g
1 S: *Green Pharmaceuticals felt they didn't have enough contacts in China.*
T: *We needed to improve things … to increase our number of contacts …*
A: *I decided to organise a pharmaceutical conference in Beijing.*
R: *In the end my hard work resulted in a successful conference, with our employees meeting and talking to the right people.*

h
Situation: at the time …
Target: we needed to …
Action: I decided to …
Result: in the end …

i
Situation: probably the best example is …; there was one time when …; the problem was …
Target: I wanted to be a bit more …
Action: so I …; I agreed to …
Result: we actually ended up …; So it all worked out in the end

k
1 A guest speaker for a conference Vicky was organising had his flight cancelled.
2 She booked another flight for the speaker. She explained the situation to the delegates and invited them to have coffee and cakes while they waited for the speaker to arrive.
3 Initiative; negotiation skills; organisational skills; communication skills. Vicky demonstrated her ability to think quickly and not panic when faced with a problem.

l
2 Anyway, what happened was
3 It was very important
4 So I decided to
5 I managed to
6 Unfortunately this meant that
7 As soon as
8 I then
9 which I'd organised beforehand
10 In the end

m
Vicky uses the past simple to give the key events of her story (*I decided, I managed, I took, I contacted* etc.). She also uses the past continuous to give background information (*I was organising*) and the past perfect to talk about something that happened before another past event (*he'd landed, I'd organised*).

n
This sentence is very visual and also humorous. It is easy to picture the conference participants happily networking, with Vicky desperately trying to persuade them to finish their coffee and cakes and go back into the main room for the opening speech. Also, by using *did arrive* rather than *arrived* she draws attention to the fact that in spite of all the problems he actually arrived. She also uses adverbs (*finally, actually*) to emphasise a pleasant surprise after a long and nervous wait.

o
1 My boss wasn't convinced that it was worth investing in India. However, my research managed to prove that in fact / actually / as a matter of fact it was.
2 As a result of my actions, what could have been a disaster in fact / actually turned out to be a big success.
3 My work had really helped, and I thought that I would be invited to join the marketing team permanently, but in fact / as a matter of fact I was actually invited to lead the team!
4 I believed my suggestions would lead to bigger profits. What I didn't expect was that in fact / as a matter of fact profits at the company would actually grow by nearly 20%!

3a
1 Probably Sabine Griffin and one or two other colleagues
2 He couldn't stand his boss.
3 To focus on the positives in every question and avoid any negatives

b
2 liked   6 position
3 working   7 develop
4 feel   8 further
5 stretched

d
1 negative   3 opportunities
2 embarrass   4 problems

e
1 b   2 c   3 a

f
a This is a common technique, but be careful as without true examples it may be too obvious that you are manipulating the question to shout about how wonderful you are. Avoid clichéd answers such as 'I'm a perfectionist'.

b This is an excellent technique as it focuses on a weakness that no longer exists. By telling a carefully prepared story you can demonstrate self-awareness, how you actively remedied the problem and developed the skills required for the position. Use the STAR method to tell a captivating story about something that didn't go as planned and describe what you would do differently next time.
c This is a safe, well-used technique. Knowledge-based weaknesses, such as a lack of technical expertise or knowledge of a language, are easily overcome and will not put the employer off giving you the job. This is especially true if you can talk about steps you have taken to remedy this weakness.

g
Candidate 1

4a
She softens the negative (*I used to procrastinate*) in this sentence by adding *sometimes* and *a little* and therefore reduces the negative impact of the information.

b
Softening: *sometimes*; *a little*; *There were times when*; *perhaps*
Emphasising: *strict*; *all*; *well*; *really*; *much*; *at the same time*

c
1 very   4 really
2 very   5 always
3 very

d
Weaknesses? Well, I can be a bit of a workaholic and always get very involved in every project that I work on. I'm happy to spend a lot of time and energy making sure that every project is as successful as possible. So, occasionally, when I feel that other members of the team might not be working as hard, I can get a little frustrated. I am aware of this problem, and I try to solve situations like this by being extremely positive and enthusiastic.

e
1 used to (*I sometimes used to procrastinate*). This emphasises that the past state or action is no longer true.
2 present perfect (*Using a schedule has really helped me*)
3 be used to + -ing (*I'm used to using Windows*); get used to + -ing (*I'd get used to using Apple Macs very quickly*)
4 can (*I can be a bit of a workaholic; I can get a little frustrated*)

f
1 I occasionally have a little difficulty making decisions.
2 I used to be a bit too stubborn and it was sometimes hard to get me to change my mind.
3 When working on projects I am a 'big picture' person. This means that from time to time I might miss some minor details.

g
1 b   2 a   3 c

h
a ever; significant; actively; even
b a lot of; every single; possible; carefully; all
c entire; successful; completely

i

Adam avoids answering this question directly and uses it as an opportunity to demonstrate that he is a positive, forward-looking individual. During interviews try not to say anything negative about your last or current job. It is much better to identify something within the post you are applying for that is different and challenging. Another positive aspect of Adam's answer is that he mentions not only what the new job can offer him, but also what he has to offer. The key word in Adam's response to this question is the word *contribute*.

j
2 d   3 c   4 f   5 b   6 a
Adam used a, c, e and f.

5c
2 f   3 b   4 a   5 e   6 c   7 g

d
1 d   2 a

6a
2 It significantly reduces the cost for the employer.
3 Financial saving; feeling more relaxed; access to research materials; no need to dress smartly
4 At a time that is convenient for you, the candidate
5 It will help you to relax and project a positive image.
6 To try and set up a face-to-face interview

c
Alex could do the following: provide a believable reason why now is not a good time for the interview; arrange another time for the interview to take place, ideally later that day; try to get the interviewer to phone him back to save unnecessary costs; make sure he is fully prepared in a quiet environment at the time he has arranged for the interview.

d
Alex handles the call well. He gives a believable reason why this is not a good time for the interview and reschedules it for later that day.

e
1 How can I help you
2 I'm very happy you called
3 What time is good for you
4 I look forward to it

f
1 Managing the logistics of theatre performances; managing performance contracts; participating in advisory panel meetings
2 Yes, there would be support from the rest of the team.
3 He is using a mobile phone and has bad reception.
4 By helping new writers finance and develop their plays

g
2 ✓   3 ✓   4 ✓   5 ✗   6 ✓   7 ✗   8 ✓

h
2 R   3 I   4 C   5 C   6 C   7 I   8 I

i
2 I didn't quite catch what you said
3 Do you mean
4 I'm having trouble hearing you. Can you hear me clearly?
5 Could you tell me what that would involve?
6 So, if I understand you correctly

Unit 6

1a
1 Send a brief thank-you letter to the employer.
2 If you haven't heard from the employer after any time agreed during the interview, or after five days if no time was agreed upon, then it is perfectly acceptable to send a brief reminder to the employer. In this letter you can repeat your interest in the position and politely enquire as to when you will be notified regarding the success of your application.
3 If you accept a position but have applied for a number of jobs, it is good practice to inform the other companies of your decision. These employers may often end up being future business contacts of yours.

b
It will help you to prepare for a second interview. If you do not get offered the job, it will help you to learn from your mistakes.

d
1 Silvia feels that the interview went well.
2 She suggests Silvia writes a follow-up letter to improve her chances of being offered the job.
3 Appearing desperate for the job

e
See Sophie's ideas in audioscript 6.2

f
Sophie's ideas:
1 It will impress the interviewer and show them that you are organised and professional. It will keep you fresh in the interviewer's mind.
2 This will demonstrate that you recognise the importance of what the interviewer said, and demonstrates good listening skills and the ability to put received information into practice.
3 This will show that you clearly understand the requirements of the job and the challenges it will bring, and that you are able to meet these challenges.
4 This will help the interviewer to clearly see you doing the job.
5 It might be the crucial deciding factor in getting you the job.

g
2 g   3 c   4 a   5 f   6 d   7 b   8 e   9 i

h
Dear Mr Lewis, // Thank you very much … Futerra is doing. // As mentioned when we met … to work in this area. // I recognise the importance … communication with key clients. // Please feel free to contact … or suitability for the position. // I look forward to … meeting me. // Yours sincerely, // Silvia Carnali

i
1 Thank you for taking the time to discuss …; I appreciate the time you and the team took in telling me about the specific aspects of the job
2 I am particularly interested in the projects that you talked about during the interview; I look forward to hearing from you
3 I am confident in my ability to meet the challenges …; I feel I am perfectly suited for …; I believe I can make a significant contribution towards …
4 Having discussed the role with you in greater depth …; I am particularly interested in the projects that you talked about during the interview; This helped me gain a better understanding of …

j
1 Thank you for taking the time to discuss
2 I appreciate the time you and the team took in telling me about the specific aspects of the job
3 This helped me gain a better understanding of
4 I feel I am perfectly suited for
5 I look forward to hearing from you

2a
2 F   3 T   4 T   5 T   6 F   7 T

3a
2 I am grateful
3 Obviously I am disappointed
4 I would very much appreciate
5 I am confident
6 Thank you very much in advance

b
Paul did not have enough work experience for the position; he failed to provide enough examples of leadership skills during the interview; his interview responses were generally too short and he failed to provide enough concrete examples to support his claims.

c
1 Paul gave several good answers in the interview, and in particular demonstrated his customer service skills well. However, generally Paul failed to provide enough evidence, through specific examples, to demonstrate other skills necessary for the position (*your answers were often short and lacking examples*).
2 To plan his answers more carefully before his next interview
3 The interviewers needed specific examples of his leadership skills – different examples are required for each skill.
4 Mr Brooker genuinely wants Paul to apply for the junior position. If Paul had not impressed Mr Brooker during the interview, it is extremely unlikely that he would have made the suggestion.

4a
1 It is important to remember when receiving a job offer that you do not have to accept it. As well as being certain that this is the right career choice for you, you need to consider a number of things including: location, travelling time, promotional prospects, perks of the job, as well as obvious salary considerations. You may like the job very much but feel you can only accept it if you are offered slightly more money, for example.
2 A formal acceptance letter, although not a written contract, is an excellent way of accepting a job. It is also an effective method of clarifying the terms and conditions as you understand them before you sign a contract and start work. Equally if you decide not to accept the position, although you do not need to specifically state why, it is good practice to write a formal letter declining the position. Even if you don't want the job now, you never know when you might be in touch with a company again. It pays to be polite.

b
Alex didn't accept the position immediately. This seems professional and gives him time to consider the offer.

c

2 position
3 salary
4 time
5 consider
6 offer
7 contact
8 decision
9 latest
10 meantime

e

1 No, he is looking forward to moving to London.
2 Yes, he could see himself working well as part of the team.
3 Yes
4 Fringe benefits (for example, holiday entitlement); whether King's Theatre will be willing to pay him while he attends a training course
5 Send a formal letter of acceptance

f

2 e 3 c 4 d 5 a

g

Dear Mr Bradshaw, // Thank you for your offer … beginning work at King's Theatre. // I am pleased to accept your offer … within my new role at King's Theatre. // During the interview … holiday leave I will be entitled to. // Thank you again for offering … the theatre team on July 29. // Yours sincerely, // Alex Mencken

h

As we discussed on the phone yesterday; As we agreed; During the interview
Other phrases: I am delighted to accept your offer and look forward to beginning work at …; I am pleased to accept your offer at a salary of … annually; I also understand that I will receive …; During the interview we did not discuss … and I hope you will be able to clarify …; I very much look forward to joining you and the … team on …

i

They personalise Alex's letter and make him sound very positive and enthusiastic about the new job.

5a

2 I'm calling as I've been offered
3 I just wanted to let you know
4 I was very impressed by your team
5 That's very kind of you
6 It's the least I could do

c

2 b 3 a 4 c 5 f 6 e

d

2 I greatly enjoyed meeting
3 I am writing to withdraw from consideration for the position
4 I have decided to accept a position elsewhere
5 closely matches my abilities and personal career aims
6 best of success

6a

1 If you decline a job offer, remember that this employer may be an important contact for you in future. Therefore it is essential that you maintain a professional, courteous relationship. Secondly, it is worth remembering that if you received a job offer from this employer, they believed in your ability to do a good job for their company, so treat them with respect. Lastly, the employer might reply to your well-written, polite letter with an even better offer.

2 It is not necessary to state whose offer you accepted, nor provide lengthy details about why you have turned down their job offer. Indeed, if you do not give specific reasons for turning down a job, this will increase your chances of receiving an improved offer.
3 If you're positive that you do not want the job, or once you have received a signed offer letter or signed contract for a job that you prefer

b

1 Future Designs
2 Ms Johnson
3 Graphic Designer
4 The work the company does, in particular the advertising campaigns for major retailers
5 Offered another job more suited to his skills and interests

c

2 spent
3 impressed
4 However
5 accept
6 opportunity

e

Suggested answers
Thank you for extending the offer for the position of …; I very much appreciate the time and effort you and your team spent …; I was very impressed by …; However, after much thought and careful deliberation, I have decided not to accept your offer; I have decided to accept another position, which …; Thank you again for your time and consideration.

7b

Nick negotiates a better deal.

c

Advice given: establish the employer's salary range for the position; remember to negotiate 'fringe benefits' like holiday entitlement, health cover, etc; try to get the employer to mention a figure first and then try to improve it; only negotiate with people who have the power to make decisions regarding salary (this may not always be the person interviewing you); establish if and when your pay will be reviewed before agreeing to any salary offers; do your research and establish the 'market rate' for similar positions; only negotiate if you are confident that you are the employer's first-choice candidate

d

1 expect
2 might
3 would
4 Could
5 Would

e

b 2 c 1 d 5 e 4 f 6

f

1 the range is for this position / the range for this position is; with my level of experience
2 would you consider a higher amount
3 current offer is below the market rate for this position

g
Student B's negotiation role play cards for Exercise 7g on page 83:

Student B: Candidate	Possible score	Actual score
Salary:		
Salary €30,000 pa	180	
For every €500 more	100	
For every €500 less	−20	
Holiday:		
25 days' holiday	100	
For every day more	20	
For every day less	−50	
Benefits:		
Company car	100	
Mobile phone	20	
Pay review in six months	10	
Total points:		

Student B: Employer	Possible score	Actual score
Salary:		
Salary €20,000 pa	300	
For every €500 more	−20	
For every €500 less	50	
Holiday:		
28 days' holiday	60	
For every day more	−40	
For every day less	50	
Benefits:		
Company car	−60	
Mobile phone	−30	
Pay review in six months	−30	
Total points:		

Preparing to apply

Your strengths and weaknesses

(Occasionally) I am …	I'm able to delegate / work independently etc.
I try to …	I would like to be able to …
I'm excellent at / (quite/reasonably) good at / (not) very good at Maths / making decisions etc.	I can (sometimes) find it difficult to make decisions / manage my time effectively etc.
I could be better at …	I can be (a little bit) indecisive / disorganised etc.
I'm interested in …	I recently managed to run a marathon / manage a project through all its stages etc.
I'm fluent in French/Spanish etc.	

Personal characteristics

creative / uncreative	flexible / inflexible	persuasive / unpersuasive
decisive / indecisive	well-organised / disorganised	reliable / unreliable

Your qualifications

I graduated from X university with a BA / an MSc etc. in Sociology/French etc.

I read English/Maths etc. at X university.

I hold a Master's degree / an MBA etc.

I was awarded a scholarship to read Business Studies / Modern Languages etc.

I have a Physics/History degree from X university, which is equivalent to a BSc/BA in Physics/History in the UK.

It was a three-year course, something like a BEd/BSc in the UK.

BA/BSc Hons (First / 2:1 / 2:2)

Transferable skills

analytical skills – identify a mistake, analyse data, conduct a survey

creativity – invent a machine, suggest an alternative, solve a problem

communication skills – write a report, explain an idea, give a presentation

interpersonal skills – resolve a dispute, listen to someone's point of view, work with 'difficult' people

negotiation skills – change someone's mind, negotiate with someone, convince someone to do something

leadership skills – chair a meeting, motivate a team, delegate tasks

organisational skills – meet deadlines, decide on priorities, implement a plan

teamworking skills – discuss an issue, contribute to a meeting, support a colleague

self-confidence	self-awareness	intelligence
resourcefulness	flexibility	intercultural awareness
independence	determination	self-motivation

Job advertisement terminology/jargon

CCDL – current clean driving licence	POS – point of sale
CV – curriculum vitae / resume	circa – about
EXP – experience	closing date – deadline for application
AGY – agency	k/K – thousand (£18k = £18,000)
OTE – on-target earnings	ref – reference number
PA – per annum (per year)	pro rata salary – salary that is calculated as a proportion of a full-time job
PW – per week	

CVs

Personal statements

(with) three years' full-time / substantial / considerable experience in managing teams / working under pressure etc.

communicate/work etc. confidently and effectively

proven ability to meet deadlines / make presentations etc.

Headings

Personal strengths and competencies
- Strategic thinking
- Innovation and creativity
- Leadership
- Flexibility
- Initiative
- Focus on results
- Teamworking
- Cross-functional working
- Organisational skills

Areas of professional experience
- Sales
- Marketing
- Presentations and publications
- Accountancy
- Electronic engineering
- Professional awards

Business skills
- Financial management
- People management / Managing people
- Dealing with customers
- Negotiation skills
- Project management
- Communication skills

Talking about your skills and experience

My role was to …

As the … I acted as …

Within this role I was responsible for leading a team of five / implementing the new strategy etc.

To do this effectively I had to …

The nature of … meant that I had to …

My past experience of … has brought me a greater understanding of … , as well as …

I implemented a new …

I believe I can apply the skills obtained from my previous employment to this position.

I worked at X for two years, where I learned that …

Working at X helped me to learn the importance of …

I have a strong history of …

I regularly …

I feel I have significantly strengthened my knowledge and understanding of …

This experience has enabled me to build on …

My employment experience leads me to the conclusion that …

I think that I could bring …

My responsibilities included …

As you can see from my CV I have …

In the course of my current job I have …

At present I am responsible for …

As a result …

While I was at … I was in charge of …

As part of my degree course in … I …

Talking about your interests

avid	sailor
dedicated	rock guitarist
committed	mountain climber
expert	reader
regular	tennis champion
former	blogger
proficient	ski instructor
successful	ballroom dancer
active	stamp collector
keen	speaker of Portuguese
qualified	volunteer
experienced	jewellery maker

Cover letters

Opening paragraph

I am a final-year student who is about to graduate from X university with a BA in Industrial Engineering.

I am writing to enquire about possible employment opportunities with …

I am interested in the position for a Marketing Executive / PA advertised in *The Guardian* newspaper / on your website.

I am writing in response to your advertisement for …

I enclose my CV for your consideration.

I was recently speaking with X and s/he recommended that I contact you / send you a copy of my CV.

Given my experience in X, s/he felt that I would be an ideal candidate for the job.

I would like to apply for the post of …

Please accept this letter as application for the Marketing Manager position currently advertised on your website.

I am writing regarding the secretarial vacancy …

Main body

My past experience of … has brought me a greater understanding of …, as well as …

As part of my degree course in … at …, I …

I am currently working as …

At present I am responsible for / in charge of …

My responsibilities include …

Since I work with …, I have developed …

I feel I have significantly strengthened my knowledge and understanding of …

I believe I can apply the skills obtained from my previous employment to this position.

I am confident that the combination of my … and … makes me an ideal candidate for the position.

This experience has enabled me to …

Working in … helped me to learn the importance of …

During … I suggested …

During my period of employment at … I gained …

I implemented a new …

These changes led to a significant increase in …

As you can see from my CV I have …

I have a strong history of …

I think that I could bring …

Final paragraph

I would appreciate the opportunity to meet you to discuss my skills, capabilities and professional experience in greater detail.

I would welcome the opportunity to discuss my professional history and qualifications with you in greater detail.

I would be happy to supply you with further references should you require them.

Should you require any further information regarding my application, please do not hesitate to contact me.

I look forward to hearing from you.

I would like to thank you in advance for your time and consideration.

Please find enclosed a copy of my curriculum vitae, which gives further details of my education and career to date.

Thank you in advance for your consideration.

Yours sincerely,

Interviews

Small talk

How are you? I'm very well, thank you.

Thank you. It's nice to meet you too / at last.

I can't believe the weather at the moment! I know. It's awful, isn't it?

Is there somewhere I could leave my umbrella? I got caught in the rain.

I'm very sorry I'm late. I was planning to be here over an hour ago, but my train was cancelled.

I was just admiring the office.

That's quite all right. / That's okay.

Do you think I could have a glass of water while I'm waiting?

Do you have a company brochure I could have a look at while I'm waiting?

Do you think I could use your toilet to freshen up?

Are there many other candidates scheduled for interviews today?

I had terrible problems parking here. Is it always this busy?

I'm afraid I'm not feeling very well. Could I sit down for a few minutes?

No thank you, I'm fine.

Talking about yourself

I am … and apply a(n) … approach to my work.	I can speak Spanish fluently / reasonably well / a little.
I believe in …	I work well under pressure / in a team / autonomously.
This enables me to …	I think I'm suitable for the position of … because …
I'm also able to …	In this way I am able to …
For example, in my last job …	I feel that I am …
In my last job I was responsible for negotiating deals / European sales etc.	I have recently started to … to improve …
I am used to dealing with customers / managing big budgets etc.	When I was at university I used to be …
	I used to be …, but I've started …, which has enabled me to …
I have a good knowledge of …	I enjoy …
	I'm a keen …

Talking about specific experiences

At the time …	I wanted to be a bit more …	I decided to …
There was a time when …	What needed to be done was …	Therefore I …
There was one situation when …	Unfortunately this meant that …	I organised a(n) …
The problem was …	It was very important that …	So in order to … I …
Probably the best example is …	It was clear that …	This resulted in …
I discovered that …	We actually ended up …	This led to …
I realised that …	Anyway, what happened was …	In the end …
I agreed to …	I managed to …	

Talking about the company

Before applying for this position / to university, I did a lot of research into …

In the end I decided to … as it was clear that …

I had a look at your website and could see that you …

I definitely feel, from everything I've learnt about …, that this is the type of organisation I'd like to work for.

You came across on your website as …

It's really something that attracted me to …

I want to work with your company because you have a really excellent/strong/outstanding reputation.

The work you do seems to be very fulfilling/worthwhile/satisfying.

I think working for you would be very enjoyable/challenging/fulfilling.

Structuring your answer

When I was at …	Ever since …	So to sum up …
… years ago	Following my degree / that etc.	
That's really when …	Firstly, … Secondly, … Finally, …	

Softening negative information

I can be a bit (of a) …	I'm keen to develop …
I can occasionally be a little …	I'm looking for an opportunity to …
I can get … at times	I feel I'm best suited to …
I occasionally have difficulty making decisions / handling criticism etc.	I'm seeking the possibility to develop further professionally.
From time to time I …	I'm seeking fresh challenges.

Emphasising positive information

I put as much effort/energy as possible into …	I am extremely/very …
I pay a lot of attention to detail.	I enjoy a great deal about my current job.
I make sure that every single …	

Clarifying

Could you explain what you mean by ...?	Could you elaborate a little on ...?
So, if I understand you correctly, ...	Could you tell me what that would involve?
Do you mean ...?	

Telephone interviews

I'm sorry, could you say that again?	I'm having trouble hearing you. Can you hear me clearly?
I didn't quite catch what you said.	

After the interview

Follow-up letter

Thank you for taking the time to discuss ...

I appreciate the time you and the team took in telling me about the specific aspects of the job.

I greatly appreciated the opportunity to meet with you and your team.

I would like to thank you for talking with me about ...

After meeting with you, I am further convinced that ...

This helped me gain a better understanding of ...

I am particularly interested in the projects that you talked about during the interview.

After the interview, I am even more excited at the prospect of ...

As mentioned when we met ...

Having discussed the role with you in greater depth ...

I am confident in my ability to ...

I feel I am perfectly suited for ...

I believe I can make a significant contribution towards ...

I look forward to hearing from you.

If you require any additional information from me in the meantime, please do not hesitate to contact me.

Requesting feedback following rejection

Obviously I am disappointed to have been unsuccessful this time ...

I would very much appreciate it if you could explain in greater detail why my application was unsuccessful on this occasion.

I am confident this information will help me to identify areas which I need to work on ...

Accepting a job offer

Thank you for your offer of employment as ...

As we discussed on the phone, I am delighted to accept your offer and look forward to starting work at ...

I am pleased to accept your offer of a starting salary of ...

As we agreed, ...

I also understand that I will ...

During the interview we did not discuss ...

I hope you will be able to clarify ...

Thank you again for offering me this wonderful opportunity.

I very much look forward to starting my employment with you on ...

Declining a job offer

I'm calling as ... / I just wanted to let you know that ...	Thank you for giving me the chance to talk about ...
I have been offered a job elsewhere, which I have accepted.	I have decided to accept a position elsewhere.
I wanted to say that I really enjoyed meeting you.	I am writing to withdraw from consideration for the position.
I was very impressed by ...	Thank you again for your time and consideration.

APPENDIX 2 Common interview questions

50 common interview questions

1 Why did you choose to study your degree subject?
2 What did you most/least enjoy about your time at university?
3 What skills did you develop at university?
4 What was the most challenging aspect of your degree course?
5 How will your degree help you in this position?
6 Tell us something about yourself.
7 What do you like doing in your spare time?
8 Why do you want this job?
9 Why should we hire you?
10 What can you bring to this position?
11 What do you consider to be the key skills necessary for this position?
12 What will you do if you don't get this job?
13 What are your strengths/weaknesses?
14 What is your biggest achievement?
15 What do you know about our company?
16 What attracted you to our company?
17 What do you think of our website?
18 Who would you consider to be our main competitors?
19 What trends are likely to affect our industry over the next few years?
20 How do you typically approach new projects?
21 Describe your management style.
22 What sorts of things do you like to delegate?
23 What qualities do you look for in a manager?
24 How do you handle stress?
25 Tell me about your ability to work under pressure.
26 In what environment do you work best?
27 What motivates you in terms of work?
28 What interests you most/least in your current work?
29 What would you change about your current job if you could?
30 Why are you considering leaving your current job?
31 Why did you leave your last job?
32 What are you looking for in a job?
33 What do you think will be the most challenging aspect of this role?
34 What kinds of decisions do you find difficult to make?
35 Tell us about a time when you demonstrated good customer service / leadership skills etc.
36 Tell us about a time when you have been innovative at work.
37 Tell us about a time you encountered a problem and how you resolved it.
38 Tell us about a time when you had to make a difficult decision.
39 Tell us about a time when you successfully managed a difficult situation at work.
40 Describe a situation in which you took a risk. What were the results?
41 How do you work in a team?
42 How would your colleagues describe you?
43 How would your manager describe your work?
44 When were you happiest at work?
45 You seem not to have too much experience in X. Do you think this would be a problem?
46 Do you think you are overqualified for this position?
47 How have you changed over the last five years?
48 Where do you see yourself in five years' time?
49 How do you hope to develop your career further?
50 Do you have any questions you would like to ask us?

Baldrick College
Swinton
SW4 8BT
natalie.laurent@bc.ac.uk

1 December 2008

Hillier and Thompson
45 Strand
London WC2 8LK

Dear Ms Ainsley,

I am writing to apply for the position of junior consultant at Hillier and Thompson advertised in *The Independent*. Having read the job description, I believe that my excellent academic record, professional experience and interpersonal skills make me a strong candidate for the position.

As a postgraduate student studying International Relations at Warsaw University, I am currently completing my MA dissertation. Prior to this I spent nine months gaining practical experience in European Public Affairs, during a paid traineeship at CLAN Public Affairs in Brussels. My primary role at CLAN was to monitor developments in the energy sector at the European Commission, and to prioritise and communicate this information in a clear and concise manner, in line with individual client needs. Whilst in Brussels I used my strong interpersonal skills to establish a wide network of contacts. This network, combined with my research and analytical skills, enabled me to identify the information our clients required rapidly and effectively. My efficiency in this role, as well as my ability to communicate clearly with clients and colleagues, lead to my promotion to team leader after only three months.

As you will see from my CV, I obtained a competitive scholarship to complete my first degree at North-eastern Illinois University, Chicago. My experiences of studying in America and working in Belgium have taught me how to live and work in diverse and challenging environments. This has helped me to work more effectively, both independently and as part of a team.

I am now looking for a position in which I can use and continue developing my professional skills. I am confident I could bring a great deal to the junior consultant position at Hillier and Thompson. Your advertisement states that the position will require close collaboration with the Central European Office in Milan, which will involve frequent trips to Italy. Having spent many previous holidays in Italy, I know the country and culture well. I have managed to acquire good conversational Italian and am currently taking evening classes to improve my language proficiency in this area. I also have fluent French following my work experience in Brussels.

Should you have any queries regarding my application, or require any further information, please do not hesitate to contact me. I would like to thank you in advance for your time and consideration.

I look forward to hearing from you.

Yours sincerely,

Natalie Laurent

Ms Natalie Laurent

Acknowledgements

The authors and publishers acknowledge the following sources of copyright material and are grateful for the permissions granted. While every effort has been made, it has not always been possible to identify the sources of all the material used, or to trace all copyright holders. If any omissions are brought to our notice, we will be happy to include the appropriate acknowledgements on reprinting

Futerra Sustainability Communications Ltd for the logo on p. 18, and for permission to base Unit 1 on their Company;

Chambers Harrap Publishers Ltd for the extract on p. 29 'Education' from *Chambers Desktop Guides, Job Applications*. Copyright © Chambers Harrap Publishers Ltd, 2006. Reproduced by permission of Chambers Harrap Publishers Ltd;

Bea Oaff for the text on p. 67 'Questions to ask' from 'Any Questions', *The Guardian*. Reproduced by permission of Bea Oaff.

Photo acknowledgements

Alamy Charles O. Cecil p12, David Davis Photoproductions p26 (t), ImageState p26 (b), blickwinkel p30
Corbis C. Devan / zefa p6, (t, m), Artiga Photo p47 (t, m), Hans Neleman p59 (t, m)
Getty Images Alex Mares-Manton / Asia Images p26 (m), Shelly Strazis / UpperCut Images p31 (t), Khalid Hawe / UpperCut Images p48 (b), Chabruken / Taxi p52, Stockbyte p73 (t, m)
iStockphoto.com Pali Rao p19 (t, m) and p34 (t, m), Ben Blankenburg p48 (t), Christine Glade p75, Justin Horrocks p83
Masterfile David Schmidt p14, Mark Leibowitz p68 (l), Jerzyworks p68 (r)
PA Photos Elizabeth Dalziel / AP p61
Photolibrary p31 (b)
Punchstock Designpics.com p10, DAJ p60

Designed and produced by eMC Design Ltd, www.emcdesign.org.uk.

Author acknowledgements

I would like to thank my editors at Cambridge University Press, especially Clare Sheridan and Jeremy Day, who provided invaluable professional expertise, support and guidance throughout the process of writing this book. I also thank Jessica Errington for all the highly valued experience and skills she brought to the preparation of the manuscript for production and printing, and for all of the many ways she has helped in the development of the book. I very much appreciate the importance of their input at every stage of the project.

The book has also benefited enormously from the very useful feedback I have received from teachers, students, colleagues and friends. I would especially like to thank Andrew Manasseh, Christine Pollefoort and Nina Hurry at the British Council Brussels, and my professors at King's College London, for their encouragement, time and guidance.

Also, as always, I am very grateful to my close friends and family for their patience and support during the writing of this book, especially Diana Allsopp.

Cambridge English for … is a new series of ESP courses for different areas of English for Specific Purposes. Written for professionals by professionals, these short courses combine the best in ELT methodology with real professional practice.

Other titles in the series: